"When the British say they love France ... it is an idea of France; of a land, as it were, of milk and honey; of lavender and olive oil and vins rouge, blanc et rosé (Peter Mayle has a lot to answer for); a land populated, if at all, by genial rustics in berets, always ready for a quick one, and beautiful women all looking like Brigitte Bardot and sounding like Juliette Greco." *Lucretia Stewart*

Packed with ideas, inspiration and 'travel intelligence' on France from top writers and journalists - hotels, hideaways, restaurants, walks, drives and much more - the BEST OF FRANCE is your first step to rediscovering the magic of France. Detailed planning chapters on websites, books and specialist operators follow each section. Whether you are a first time visitor or an experienced francophile, our aim is to stimulate new ways to get the most from this favourite destination.

Some of these articles, as well as thousands of others, can be seen online at WWW.TRAVELINTELLIGENCE.NET

Anthology copyright © 2002 Travel Intelligence Ltd. All written material authors' copyright. For image and additional credits, see final pages.

Travel Intelligence Ltd does not guarantee the accuracy or suitability of any advice given in this publication, and cannot be held liable for any errors or omissions. You are strongly advised to check practical details in advance of making travel plans, because these can change frequently and without warning.

Edited, with section introductions, by
Jamie Dunford Wood
Designed by
Jamie Dunford Wood
Editorial Director
AA Gill
Assistant Editor
Lucy E. Judkins
Editorial Assistants
Jenny Pidgeon
Allyson Benavidez

Travel Intelligence contributing writers

Alf ALDERSON   Sarah ANDERSON   Rose BARING
Maureen BARRY   Richard BINNS   Dea BIRKETT   John
BORTHWICK   Greg BREINING   Tom BROSNAHAN
(commissioning editor, US)   Sue CARPENTER   David
CLEMENT-DAVIES Joe CUMMINGS Ben CURTIS William
DALRYMPLE   Andrew EAMES   Catherine FAIRWEATHER
AA GILL (editorial director)   Robin HANBURY-TENISON
Justine HARDY   Fraser HARRISON   John HATT   Anthony
HEALY   James HENDERSON   Mark HUDSON   Rupert
ISAACSON   Brian JACKMAN   Steve JERMANOK   Tom KAY
Jim KEEBLE   Steven KNIPP   Nancy LYON   Rory MACLEAN
Philip MARSDEN (commissioning editor, UK)   Lee
MARSHALL   Gregory McNAMEE   Mark MCCRUM   Kamin
MOHAMMADI   Kate MORRIS   Andrew MUELLER   Martin
O'BRIEN   Rob PENN   Barnaby ROGERSON   Melissa ROSSI
Anthony SATTIN   Dan SCOTT   Jeremy SEAL   Jasper SHARP
Christopher SOMERVILLE   Rory SPOWERS   Lucretia
STEWART   Stanley STEWART   Susan STORM   Sean THOMAS
Nigel TISDALL   Isabella TREE   Yvonne VAN DONGEN   Vitali
VITALIEV   Binyavanga WAINAINA   John WARBURTON-LEE
Sara WHEELER   Simon WINCHESTER   Jasper WINN
Stuart WOLFENDALE

The Best of France

ISBN 1-904131-05-0

published by Travel Intelligence Ltd / Lockwood Publishing
2 Oaklands Grove, London W12 0JA United Kingdom

For information on Travel Intelligence's other products and
services, please visit **www.travelintelligence.net**
or email i@travelintelligence.net

Contents

CONTENTS

Lucretia Stewart

———

I first went to France one summer when I was about ten. My parents were keen that I should learn French. They sent me to board with a Monsieur and Madame Malard - I don't know how they found them, but they were perfect. Monsieur Malard was a small, bald, downtrodden man with a wispy moustache; Madame was rather like Hyacinth Bucket in "Keeping Up Appearances". They lived in a big old house in Warmeriville, a small village near Rheims. Xavière, their tomboyish granddaughter, who was a couple of years older than me, had come to spend the holidays with them, and it was assumed that we would be company for each other. It didn't seem to matter that I couldn't speak French. Anyhow, I soon could. All summer long she and I ran contentedly wild together, out most of the day, exploring the countryside on bicycles, playing in the garden, telling stories late into the night.

I can only remember fragments of my stay there, snapshots. For instance, dinner always began with soup, and, if Xavière and I got hungry in the afternoon, we were given slabs of dark chocolate on bread. We drank our milky breakfast coffee (children, coffee, imagine) from bowls. The vegetable garden, where all the vegetables we ate grew, was full of huge slugs ("limace") and snails (which were called "limaçon," rather than "escargot"). I hated both. Once, out bicycling along the towpath by the river, we met some rough boys who pulled our hair and clothes. They let us go just as

I was about to hit one of them over the head with a bottle.

After a month in the country I went to Paris for four weeks to stay with a glamorous and rather scary friend of my father, the Princesse Jeanne-Marie de Broglie, who lived in flat off the Champs-Elysées. Jeanne-Marie, who was divorced, wore wonderful couture clothes (by Balenciaga - it was nearly twenty years before I understood the full implications of this name) and smelt divine and didn't much like children, though she had two of her own.

They were older than me and off doing their own thing. As a result, I spent most of my days with their governess, seeing the sights - the Eiffel Tower, the Louvre, the Arc de Triomphe, walking in the Jardin des Tuileries, all the while having my French grammar corrected and perfected by Mademoiselle. Then I went back to Warmeriville for another month and took up where I had left off, tearing round the countryside on bicycles with Xavière. By the end of the summer, I could speak French fluently. A couple of years later, when my family had moved to Washington D.C., I went back to France with an American school friend, but it wasn't the same. Monsieur and Madame Malard hadn't changed, but Xavière wasn't there and I didn't have nearly as much fun.

But this early introduction to the two faces of France, on the one hand, deeply rural, on the other, urban and immensely chic, this glimpse into two totally opposing French worlds left me with a deep affection for and attraction to things French. I was fascinated by the glamour of Paris (who wasn't?), but I also loved the countryside.

I still can't resist the lure of Paris. I return to grimy London, refreshed and restored by the galleries, the museums (there is always at least one exhibition you want to see), the cinemas, the shops (BETTER, CHEAPER) and the restaurants (BETTER, CHEAPER). In Paris, I feel 'mondaine' - sophisticated, in control. Here I feel chaotic. This, I think, is partly because the British seem to set little store by efficiency, while, in France, everything seems to work. The trains are better; the Metro is superb (the fastest, most efficient and silent in the world, with stops never more than five minutes' walk from any destination); there are more public lavatories, often with an attendant (this is according to a friend who has recently moved to Paris; she also claims that, in Paris, "even nerds are good-looking"), and so on and so forth. I like the way eating is taken so seriously, the way almost everything closes for lunch between midday and 2.30. I even like the way French people smoke so much. There's something almost heroic about the dedication they bring to it.

I also like the notion of an intellectual life, something that, in England, is generally ridiculed or regarded with deep suspicion. The idea of it is possibly more romantic than the reality, which can seem rather self-important. The French language is geared to hyperbole, formality and waffle. Only in France would you be able to listen to an hour-long radio discussion about the correct way to pronounce Bach (eventually they concluded that "Bach" should be pronounced in the German way, but that the composer's first names should be Frenchified, thus "Jean Sebastian"). I once attended a conference in Caen in which the American writer, Edmund White, was taking part; its subject was "Écrire, Aimer." Many distinguished French intellectuals sat around till the early hours discussing literature and censorship and the difficulties of showing love (except they meant sex) on the screen. Their view was that all censorship was bad.

7

Afterwards we all went to a screening of Genet's *Chant d'Amour*, a film so explicit that you'd be lucky, even nowadays, to see it in an upstairs room in Soho.

And in the countryside, I love the markets brimming with fruit and vegetables and myriad exotic, unknown cheeses and foie gras and magret de canard and thirty different kinds of saucisson; I love particularly the old people, with their bright, weather-beaten faces, flushed from many glasses of Calvados, who come into town from their farms on market day, put up a little stall and stand behind it, sometimes selling just a few eggs, some pots of homemade jam, a rabbit or duck killed the previous afternoon, home-grown Jerusalem artichokes, carrots or leeks - whatever is in season - and, often, a straggly posy of Christmas roses or narcissi, picked early that morning.

I love the wide, open spaces. Normandy, where my aunt has a cottage, is one of those huge areas of France that is suffering from depopulation, but it is rare to feel crowded anywhere in the entire country except, perhaps, in the ancient Marais district of Paris on a Saturday. People talk about the "big" sky of Montana, but Normandy has its own vast heaven.

The English passion for France is difficult to analyse precisely. A friend married for over thirty years to a French wife describes it as a "sibling relationship." I made a list recently of the things that I thought the British liked about France.

Its proximity is a major plus. Yes, it's true it takes a day to get there, but then it almost invariably takes a day to get anywhere. Then there's the fact that it's so cheap, at least compared to England, and what you get for money is so much more and so much better.

And then there is the mysterious lure of the British notion of France, which seems to be made up of the sense that the quality of life is better, that life is generally more agreeable in France. In Nancy Mitford's novel *Don't Tell Alfred*, Grace de Valhubert is an Englishwoman married to a very attractive Frenchman. Having endured many stormy passages during the early years her marriage (the result of the difference between the two cultures more than anything else: an earlier novel, *The Blessing*, describes Grace's tribulations), Grace has now settled down and "Everything French was considered by her [Grace] superior to its English equivalent."

When I think of what the British people who have either gone to live in France or who have houses there like about it, the phrase "the good life" comes to mind. I don't mean the television programme, (though as I watch my aunt's neighbour Marcel digging his vegetable garden and listen to him proudly announce that everything they eat is "bio" - "biologique" is the French word for "organic"- I am reminded of it). I mean more an idea of a good life where food is cheap, plentiful and delicious, where there is wine with every meal, and where the gendarmes take no interest in how much you had at lunch. The British have more in common with the Americans than we might wish to acknowledge and our attitudes towards alcohol (and sex) are so complicated by feelings of guilt and distaste that we marvel at and envy the way the French apparently take such matters in their stride. Unlike the British, the French like to flirt in public (I like the way men stare boldly at me in the street), but there are rarely sex scandals in France. Your private life is just that. Private.

When the British say they love France, when they dream,

as I do, of a little house somewhere in the French country-side, I am not altogether convinced that they really love a real place. Instead it is an idea of France; of a land, as it were, of milk and honey; of lavender and olive oil and vins rouge, blanc et rosé (Peter Mayle has a lot to answer for); a land populated, if at all, by genial rustics in berets, always ready for a quick one, and beautiful women all looking like Brigitte Bardot and all sounding like Juliette Greco. Really, however, they'd prefer France if there were no people in it. I'm not much better than them. I do actually like the French, but I suspect that I love their country as much for what it represents to me - perhaps an idyllic place in my memory or in my dreams as for the qualities it actually possesses.

Romantic France

Romantic France

Romance and France means Paris. Corny to say so, but it is still true that Paris is *the* romantic city of the world. Hong Kong may have its sunsets, Sydney its beaches, Venice its piazza; but nowhere has sidewalk cafés or garret hotels or night-time illuminations like the 'city of light'.

Above all it is romantic for the English. Historically, everything naughty, dangerous, forbidden, and illicit is looked for in Paris, such a short hop across the Channel but such a long distance away across the world of the senses. In the past it was much more about sex than perhaps it is today, mixed with that heady brew of bohemia nurtered by the great artists and writers of the Edwardian era. What remains is a romantic hangover - part myth, to be sure, but no less powerful for that.

Today it is a much more comfortable city to visit than it was a century ago. The Eurostar has made it available as a lunch destination, a raft of small 'boutique' hotels have sprung up to replace the grimy walk-up hotels of old, and its metro is still clean, fast and cheap, in such contrast to

London's. Architecturally, too, it feels accessible - in the late 19th Century the old medieval quarters and slums and narrow lanes were swept away in an orgy of reconstruction under the direction of Baron Haussman, and what emerged was a city of wide tree lined boulevards, spacious sidewalks, formal parks, and classically proportioned apartment buildings of no more than eight or so stories. Unless you are a regular visitor it is hard to know where you are in the city simply by the look of the neighbourhood, because each one looks the same to the untrained eye: grey stone, balconied windows, manicured plane trees, mansard roofs.

Paris has a wealth of culture unparalleled north of the Alps - and not just the Louvre, but a host of smaller museums and galleries from the Picasso to the Rodin to the Musce D'Orsay. But more than this it is the city of romance because the visitor is able to associate themselves with a quality of life that is entirely different; French breakfasts in sidewalk cafés, browsing in little boutiques, lounging in magnificent gardens and parks. Perhaps no longer quite such a city of poets, writers and artists, it was their spiritual home for more than a century, living a life to which many of us aspire. It is the echo of that, the spirit, that remains, despite the consumerism and the queues and the tour buses and the (often) lousy food. Above all it's close, and it's cheap, and no Englishman or woman can feel what it is to be English before they have tested their Englishness against the Frenchness of Paris. Like a mistress, it's where they go to be romantic.

Stanley Stewart

In Outer Mongolia I had plenty of time to think about Paris. In nomads' tents, over yet another bowl of sheep entrails, it is remarkable how often one's thoughts turn to the Boulevard Saint-Germain and the Café de Flore. In these wild regions, Paris stood for Civilisation, and more crucially, for Love. I think I must have been lonely. To lessen the monotony of long hours in the saddle we took turns telling stories. My translator came up with the idea of 'Describing A Romantic Evening.' She conjured a hot date in Ulan Bator, the capital, that included a white limousine, a bouquet of roses, a boyfriend in a dinner jacket, and a visit to the ballet.

Anyone familiar with the grim realities of Ulan Bator will admire the vigour of her imagination. The horseman was more of a realist. A swarthy chap with a cauliflower nose, he didn't even bother with a date. His romantic evening was a bunch of his mates, a bottle of hooch and a moonlit night in a wood. The latter was his only concession to romantic flight of fancy. Mongolia is largely treeless.

My evening was in Paris, indulging all the city's romantic clichés. Sunset would be enjoyed from the steps of Sacré Coeur with all Paris spread beneath our feet. There would be champagne cocktails at Harry's Bar, a performance of Madam Butterfly at the Opera Garnier, dinner at La Coupole, a late night tango bar off the Boulevard de Sebastopol, an even later night dance hall in Bastille, and finally a walk along the banks of the Seine at dawn beneath the Pont des Arts and the Pont Neuf. My jacket would be thrown over my shoulder. My date, carrying a rose bought from an itinerant flower seller, would have taken off her shoes. An accordion would be playing somewhere. Dawn would be seeping into the sky beyond the spires of Notre Dame. We would say foolish things that would change our lives.

Back home, I couldn't wait to get to Paris. Rather conveniently, my own Love Interest happened to be there. It was a dangerous moment, time to turn fantasy into reality. I caught the 12:55 from Waterloo.

The literary tradition is daunting, and not exactly strong on happy endings. The romantic failures in the City of Love would fill a library: Héloise and Abélard, Flaubert, de Laclos, Stendhal, Proust, Victor Hugo, Henry Miller, Scott Fitzgerald. Good-time guy Samuel Beckett spent his life in Paris; his plays are hardly an advertisement for healthy human relationships.

I stepped down from the train with some trepidation.

She was waiting at the gate in the Gare du Nord, and all seemed right with the world. I hadn't seen her for six months. She looked fabulous in a beret and a leather jacket. For a romantic weekend in Paris, the Mermaid was appropriately inappropriate: beautiful, flighty, inconstant, in a word, a bombshell. I was always waiting for her to explode.

We booked into a charming little hotel opposite Notre Dame full of engravings of Victor Hugo's Esmeralda in bed with a goat. In the back office sat a remarkable Parisian apparition, La Madam, a grand dame complete with pet poodle, cigarette holder, and something dead around her shoulders. A rapid turnover of strikingly handsome young men worked her front desk. What Madam didn't know about amour was not worth knowing. She gave us a room with a view of the cathedral, an outside key to allow for late revelries, and a word of advice: the Moroccan cleaners tended to ignore the Do Not Disturb sign.

Things got off to a rocky start. The steps of Sacré Coeur, swarming with coach loads of day-trippers and battalions of tacky souvenir sellers, are more like the Tourist Experience from Hell than a romantic interlude. At the opera it turned out it would have been easier to have been taken on as the leading tenor than to get a ticket. The tango bar was closed, Harry's was full of solid American businessmen, long on loud conversations about the futures market, short on whispered endearments, and the weather seemed a trifle chilly for bare feet.

But love is about improvisation and I was not to be put off. It was early autumn. The days were clear and bright and in the Jardin du Luxembourg the leaves were gathering round the feet of young lovers from the Sorbonne, who shared benches and secrets. Outside the cafés down the rue Saint Michel, people were sitting in the sun watching the procession of cruising flaneurs.

For the English, Eurostar has meant that Paris has replaced Brighton as the rendezvous of infidelity. British life is immeasurably improved by this fact; prim Georgian terraces overlooking a grey sea is hardly a setting for passion. In Paris infidelity is part of the fabric of life. There is even a time of day devoted to it - *cinq à sept* - the hours of the mistress, neatly slotted in between the work day and the return to evening domesticity. In France politicians are not pilloried in the tabloids for having affairs; it is expected of them. No sensible French voter would want to trust the

running of the country to a man without a mistress.

In Paris even intellectuals are great lovers. Jean Paul Sartre, not exactly leading man material, went through lovers like a packet of Gauloises in spite of a lifelong relationship with Simone de Beauvoir. For her part she threw herself into serial passions with men and women alike without anyone thinking the worse of her.

We started our romantic weekend with a couple of breakfasts. We both loved Parisian breakfasts so much that we generally tried to fit two of them into a morning. From there it was a short run to lunch at the Café de l'Industrie. The name may not inspire but le Café de l'Industrie on the edge of Bastille is one of those illusive French cafés that feature in 1930s photographs of Paris: couples on the verge of embrace, caught reflected in mirrors advertising pastis. There were plants and plain wooden tables and old photographs of French actors with handlebar moustaches and waitresses who looked like they moonlighted as artists' models. You felt, if they took their kit off, you might recognise them from the Musee d'Orsay. All around us bohemian couples were engaged in discreet tête a têtes. We shared a pitcher of claret and plates of charcuterie and salad.

It was the kind of Parisian lunch I had dreamed about in Mongolia while gnawing on marmot bones.

Paris is a city for walking, for diving into the maze of back streets, and for the sweet illusion of lovers that what you find and do is found and done for the first time. In the Place Lépine we bought great bunches of lilies and tiny cactus plants, one of the Mermaid's odder passions, to fill our room. We went to see films on wet afternoons in empty cinemas, French films with lots of rather tortured people agonising about love and smoking too much. We shopped for antiques in the Place des Vosges, the finest square in Europe where 17th century husbands fought murderous duels with their wives' lovers. Near Palais Royal, a den of debauchery in the 18th century, we found a wonderful salon de thé, A Priori Thé, in the marble arcades of the Galerie Vivienne which we happily believed was unknown to anyone but ourselves and a handful of very thin French women. We bought lingerie we couldn't afford in the tiny boutiques off Place des Victories and cheese and fruit and chocolate macaroons in the markets of rue Moufftard where Hemingway enjoyed the sweet innocence of his first years in a garret with his wife. We went to an exhibition of the 18th century romantic painter Prud'hon in the Petit Palais, a series of love allegories, soft-focus theatricality full of bosomy young women and mischievous cupids, in which Love and Reason were seen as mortal enemies. We savoured the bedroom scenes and ignored the message.

When we emerged the Eiffel Tower seemed to be holding up the draperies of the descending dusk.

Whichever way you look at it, the phallic Tower is a monument to Love. It is a little known fact that the designer, Georges Eiffel, was also the designer of the garter belt. Turn the Tower upside down and the connection is obvious.

One afternoon we went to the racetrack on the grounds that there's something sexy about horses and throwing money away. It was a quiet meeting at Longchamps with small groups of serious men in caps drifting about the grandstands. We watched the horses in the parade ring, leggy and smooth-flanked and snorting hot breath into the chill afternoon, and chose our bets on the basis of their names. In the four o'clock Heart's Delight romped home at seven to one with our hundred francs riding on him, and we treated ourselves to a bottle of champagne in the China Club, a sophisticated joint in the Bastille that is a cross between a colonial club and an opium den.

On Sunday afternoon we took the train to Joinville. Before the First War middle-class Parisians came to Joinville to dance in the riverside cafes to the sweet sounds of the accordion. Chez Gégène, an old fashioned dance hall specialising in the bal musette, is the one of the only survivors of this Parisian tradition. We ate mussels and salad overlooking the banks of the Marne then went through to the dance hall where a band of accordions and violins were starting an energetic tango. The dancers had dyed hair, pale complexions, and gold necklaces, and that was only the men. The women wore full skirts and frilly blouses and hairdos that were a serious threat to the ozone layer. Everyone was in post-lunch high spirits. The Mermaid taught me to waltz, leading me gingerly through the immaculate couples. We laughed too much and bumped into people and I can't remember how we got home.

On the last evening we went to La Coupole. It was the Mermaid's birthday. The oysters came on trays of crushed ice borne by waiters in waistcoats and long aprons. I had secretly ordered a birthday cake and it made a grand theatrical entrance. The lights in the whole restaurant were dimmed and the cake, gleaming with candles, floated above the dark tables, between the fat columns, past the fountain, to arrive in front of her as the whole restaurant broke into Happy Birthday. Her eyes shone. She closed them to make a wish. I watched her eyelids fluttering as if she was dreaming. She seemed blissfully happy. Then she opened her eyes and blew out the candles in one go.

But I was wrong; she wasn't happy. On the banks of the

Seine, when all Paris seemed to have gone to sleep and the great boulevards were ghostly silent, she informed me that she felt it would be better if we parted. It was one of those moments when everything seems to stand still. The clochard urinating underneath the Pont des Arts seemed to pause in midstream and the dog on the quay stopped scratching his fleas and stared. My heart was pounding. I don't remember her reasons - something about my long absence in Mongolia and another man. Next morning I went back to the Gare du Nord, a changed man.

Three days later, she telephoned me in London. Her call was tearful. She had made a mistake. She could not live without me. In the background I could hear the bustle of a cafe, the hiss of a coffee machine. I felt I could smell our breakfast croissants.

I wasn't convinced. Perhaps the break was for the best.

"We'll always have Paris," I heard myself saying.

General online information on Paris

paris.org
The Paris Pages - very well organised and comprehensive site covering everything there is to know about Paris. There are more than 7000 pages of information on tourist companies, embassy and consular services, hotels, restaurants, events, museums, transport, discussion groups, monuments, cafes, shops, historic maps and more.

paris-touristoffice.com
Official website of Paris, packed with information.

City breaks and Hotels

Kirker Holidays
A specialist in city and short break holidays. Kirker is a small, family-run and extremely knowledgeable travel operator who caters for the quality end of the short holiday market. They pride themselves on seeking out lesser known, interesting hotels with character and style, and research all their recommendations personally. Contact them on 020 7231 3333. When asked to recommend 6 of the most romantic hotels in Paris, owner Christopher Kirker suggested:

Hotel du Quai-Voltaire
19 quai Voltaire, 7th arr. Slightly faded but well-loved hotel with great character and location, and one of the best views in Paris onto the Seine. (2*)

Libertel Quartier Latin
9 rue des Ecoles, 5th arr. Very Parisian and arty boutique hotel with a literary atmoshere just off Boulevard Saint-Germain. (3*)

Le Notre-Dame Hotel
1 Quai Saint Michel, 5th arr. Beautifully renovated 3* hotel with views over the Seine and the cathedral.

Pavillion de la Reine
28 Place des Vosges, 3rd arr. The Times has called this "arguably the prettiest and most romantic hotel in Paris". Lovely historical building. (4*)

Lancaster
7 rue de Berri, 8th arr. Very beautiful former gentlemen's residence just off the Champs Elysees where Dietrich lived, with a great residents-only restaurant. (Deluxe)

Plaza Athéné
25 Avenue Montaigne, 8th arr. One of the best hotels in Europe, if not the world, with the only Michelin 3* restaurant in Paris. A Great Palace hotel. (Deluxe)

Further Useful Links

These links might also prove useful when planning a romantic holiday in Paris or elsewhere in France:

france-exclusive.com
Useful selection of practical planning links on Paris and other French regions - restaurants, hotels, museums and lifestyle.

ticketavenue.com
Booking agent for the cabaret, theatre, opera, ballet, concerts, museums and other events.

www.gourmetsociety.com
A wide selection of the restaurants in France, including a section on the most romantic, bookable online.

Stanley Stewart's Paris

Café de Flore 172, Boulevard Saint-Germain;
Tel: +33 1 45 48 55 26; www.café-de-flore.com

La Coupole 102 Blvd. du Montparnasse; Tel: +33 1 43 20 14 20

A Priori Thé 35-37 Galerie Vivienne; Tel: +33 1 42 97 48 75

Harry's Bar 5, Rue Daunou; Tel: +33 1 42 61 71 14
Legendary birthplace of the Bloody Mary, renowned for serving
the best dry martinis in town.

China Club 50, Rue de Charenton; Tel: +33 1 43 43 82 02

Opera: www.opera-de-paris.fr
Official site of the Palais Garnier and the Bastille opera for
programme details and online reservations.

Dance lessons: www.danse-a-2.com
There are many tango bars in Paris - look here for listings of bars
and tango lessons throughout the country.

Racing: www.france-galop.com
Going to a race at the famous Longchamp Hippodrome is still a
social occasion. Find out race times here or in the Paris Turf
newspaper.

Recommended Reading

**A Guide to France for Loving Couples; The 31 Most Romantic
Hotels and Inns in France** by Cynthia Proulx. Auerbach
Publishers. ISBN: 0877690596

**Water-Mill Inns of France: A Gastronomic Guide to Romantic
Country Inns** by Marv Luther. Corinthian. ISBN: 0964908549

Special Places to Stay: Paris Hotels by Alastair Sawday.
Alastair Sawday Publishing. ISBN: 1901970132

Walking Paris: Thirty Original Walks in and Around Paris
(2nd Ed) by Giles Desmons. McGraw Hill - NTC.
ISBN: 0844201413

Through the Windows of Paris: Fifty Unique Shops
by Micheal Webb. Balcony. ISBN: 1890449024

The Cafes of Paris: A Guide
by Christine Graf. Interlink Publishing Group. ISBN: 1566562783

**The Piano Shop on the Left Bank: Discovering a Forgotten
Passion in a Paris Atelier**
by Thad Carhart. Random House. ISBN: 0375503048

Parisians: Photographs by Peter Turnley by Peter Turnley,
Adam Gopnik. Abbeville Press, Inc. ISBN: 0789206501

France Off-Piste

France Off-Piste

France is a driving country 'par excellence'. With a few exceptions - the périphérique in Paris, the Côte d'Azur in summer, and seasonal queues of British cars battling each other for parking spots in pretty Provençal villages - the vast interior of the country is blissfully light on traffic and made for that fast disappearing past-time, the motoring holiday.

Here are a few facts you may not be aware of: France is more than twice as big in land mass as the United Kingdom. It contains 24% of all agricultural land in use in the EU (just under 60% of France's total land area) and the largest forested area of any country on mainland europe. Over half a million miles of road criss-cross the country, including 4000 miles of motorway. Motorways - autoroutes - are comfortable to drive on over vast swathes of the country. However they can be expensive on tolls, and one of the joys of France is the ability to be able to detour on Routes Nationales - free and, if you're not in a hurry, allowing you glimpses of the interior of France that you would not otherwise get.

Richard Binns' classic 'Run to the Sun' itinerary allows you to drive from north to south, Calais to St Tropez, without pay one sou in tolls, with plenty of ideas for atmospheric and good value places to eat and sleep. It is republished below as a testament to one of Britain's foremost and popular writers on France. What he and his many fans have discovered is that France is brim full with charming old manor houses and chateaux to break the journey with, many snatched from ruin to be turned into hotels and bed and breakfast accommodation. Justine Hardy compares their eccentricities, while Andrew Eames discovers that even the old aristocrats are at it. With the industrialization of agriculture since the war, times have become increasingly hard for the rural economy of France. We are the beneficiaries.

Justine Hardy

ALONG THE PÉAGE

It is almost as if there was some divine Francophile plan that caused the châteaux builders to cast their eyes across the land and visualise the roaring paths of the péages. How neat that you just take a turn, a couple more, and then there is the sign 'Château Plein de Charm - not very many hundred metres', the words prettily illuminated with bunches of grapes, promises of agréable, bon confort or even confort raffiné. Sometimes the promises may be a little hollow and the veneer on the reproduction furniture a touch too thin, the pillows a bit hard and the sauces reduced just too far, but other times it is all run as if Madame La Duchesse had just left for a quick flurry to Versailles to teeter amongst the courtesans.

How the Englishman sighs when he finds bon confort just five minutes from his wrestling match with the supersonic speeds and machismo flexing of the fast lane. You just do not find quite the same thing nestling off junction 6 of the M4 out of London or indeed cupped in a curve off the ausfahrt on the A3 headed for Dusseldorf. These little châteaux, manoirs and relais sit at the end of drives - some set in park land, others seeming to sit in the middle of fields, some with fat-bellied turrets, others with perfect 18th century symmetry; or perhaps just a grand farmhouse with the chickens still on the loose, or gilded and garlanded like an opera set. When I have picked right, Madame has always been much in evidence, being discreet with lovers and attentive to loners, always offering a free hand with pillows and gourmet menu advice.

It is not even as if they are a great trade secret, shared only by the top echelon of travellers with expensive tastes and matching decks of credit cards. These are within the budget of everyone prepared to spend moderately on good living wanting respite from the rush and the hurry. They appear to prickle across the French countryside, dotting the road maps with promises of elegant furniture carefully placed around huge, sparse rooms, deft service during long dinners with great deference shown to both the palate and the digestion; for it is always the foie and the national terror of maladie de foie that seem to govern the menu planning.

They have been pushed to the limit. There was a Christmas morning that had been spent in moody progress through unfestive gloom and fog on the N6. There had been an escape from a former residence of Cistercian monks, near Nuits-St-George, where Madame had a penchant for sticking to monastic strictures to an almost perverse extent. We had been barracked into our rooms on Christmas morning until released for a stale breakfast amongst sad-eyed fellow tourists in the Yuletide vortex. But a bolt up the N6 found redemption at a manor house near Rémy. Madame Sanitas could not have been further from the maniacal Madame of Nuits-St-George. She plumped us up over tea and then sent us off around the little park to recover from road trauma and visions of mad monks. Christmas began with the sheer joy of having not so much as a miniature mince pie in sight, nor the string of elderly relatives with wet lips and sherry breath. Salmon baked in tarragon and cray fish tails with basil in filo pastry do not sit on the stomach in the same way as most festive fare.

Or there was the time when the Périphérique had been beyond endurance and Fontainbleau had offered a cold cheek. So on to Villeneuve La Dondagre to the hostellerie where the rooms were named after rubicund opera characters. After six courses and much fine wine the Spanish girls on the wallpaper in the Carmen bedroom danced like dervishes. This time Madame had created a journey through provençal cuisine, taking in grilled goats cheese and sliced artichokes, rascasse in court bouillon with coriander, tarragon sorbet with marc de Provence, baby rabbit roasted with rosemary in olive tapenade and airy millefeuille with Roquefort. Somehow it was balanced so that it was possible to squeeze in a tiny pot of dark chocolate spiked with orange and lemon zest, a strawberry sorbet and lavender and honey ice cream; all so delicately laid upon the plate as to be no threat to a bulging girth.

There was a tennis court hidden in the old kitchen garden, a swimming pool beside the parterre, a private terrace outside the room of the spinning Carmen for breakfast in the sun. There were only five other guests, so it was possible to swim with the same energy as the bacchanalian dancers on the wall paper in order to start on the next gourmet tour that Madame had lined up. As a mental 'amuse gueule' she led us through the herb garden and gave elegant descriptions of just how each variety was used in her kitchen. The only thing that seemed strange on that warm September night was the roaring fire in the hall outside the dining room. Then came the kitchen boy bearing a huge ham. He set it on a spit and spent the following hours dripping a mixture of honey and herbs over it, patiently turning it by hand while the honey blackened and bubbled.

Another potent draw to these places is their breakfasts.

We have all become so numbed by the croissant invasion of Europe that our standards seem tricky to reach, and it is rare to find a French breakfast as we feel it should be, according to our bastardized Euro-café examples; often the croissants are jaded and the brioches drier than a mouth of Kleenex. The simple truth is that frou-frou pâtisseries are not really the staple French breakfast at all. When you are presented with a basket of warm bread, home-made preserves and bowls of thick coffee it seems not to matter at all. Quite a few of them do their own baking, and if they do make croissants they crumble for the expectant audience and the brioche puff and pout as they should.

But it is not just the kitchens that make these places the havens that we so long to find. It is a formula made up of the architecture, the space in the bedrooms, the charm of the Mesdames or even the recalcitrance of some of the waiters; it is the old park land that they are set in or the village that they back on to, the smell of roses through your bedroom window or the fact that the coffee is so strong that it gives you wide open eyes for four hours afterwards; the lack of fellow guests or the roar of a Gallic row in the next room. One of the primary charms is that there is no need to grit your teeth and scream through the night, tailing the red snake and hurtling towards the white light rush, nor make a great detour to find a respite from the road.

For every good find there is another that will fill you with horror, like the monk-mad Madame in Nuits-St-George; the place where the furniture was covered in cling film and the food just as thick in aspic; the time when the brioche were not so much Kleenex as escapees from an arms depot and the one where the resident cats made love and war all night.

The safest way to avoid disasters is to know what you

want and then ring and find out if they have it or anything close to your needs. Every book shop now has several of the glossy guides that cover the ins and outs of châteaux hopping, the most succinct probably being Relais and Châteaux, produced by the people who give the places their confort grading, though be wary as they frequently soar into verbal orbit in advertorial fashion.

A twenty-four hour gap between a meeting and your return, a day's delay in getting home at the end of a holiday, a long week end or just a short escape in the middle of a grey week - all good reasons to find a châteaux off the main drag. If there is no reason to stop and stay, try to invent one, because it seems a sad omission to waste the divine intervention that plopped the péages around so many fine hostelleries, manoirs and châteaux.

Andrew Eames

The Comte Bernard de Jouffroy Gonsans, sallow, stooped and deeply courteous, had the air of someone who knew his Baudelaire; he may have been born with the proverbial silver spoon, but his back had been bent by life's ups and downs. He commiserated with our difficult journey to the dead centre of France on a hot and busy August weekend.

"La folie" he exclaimed, and graciously excused himself once he had shown us the way up with winding stone staircase, into the tower; he had a couple of racehorses to feed.

It is surprisingly easy to invite oneself to stay with the French aristocracy. No society contacts, funny handshakes or certificates of pedigree required - only a certain cheek and a thick handbook called 'Le B&B'. Being an outrageous social climber I'd scanned the book for hosts who a) had a title, b) lived in a castle and c) didn't actually say they objected to children.

The Château de la Commanderie, besides matching all those criteria, has to rank as one of the most impressive B&Bs in the world. This huge, imposing turreted mansion south-east of the Loire Valley was founded in the 11th century as a base for Knights Templar - crusader mercenaries. The Comte's family had been in residence for 300 years, but his daughters had lost the taste for castle-dwelling, so Comte Bernard was to be the last of the line, and it plainly made him sad.

Nor did his eyes exactly light up as our two tumbled, wittering, out of the car and mucked up the gravel on his driveway, which had obviously just been carefully raked. But if he had any misgivings he was far too well bred to let them show.

The B&B idea was intended to help meet the château running costs. At 74 the Comte, after several nasty falls from the saddle, had found himself unable to maintain a big racing stable, so his wife had redecorated seven rooms in the north wing with velvets, copies of Paris Match and books about Queen Elizabeth and Genghis Khan.

Very few of his visitors were French. In the evening, he and the Countess usually sat down to dinner with the assembled company, for which English would be the lingua franca. And what was usually discussed? "Oh, politics, wine, the economy, the world". Not much, then.

Our two, at four and six, are still under-informed on politics and wine, not to mention the economy and the world - I blame the parents - so I asked that we be excused from the formal part of the evening. Could we, perhaps, have a picnic in his garden instead?

There can't have been many occasions when tomato ketchup has been so liberally applied to hotdogs in the shadow of those crusader turrets. Fortunately, it wasn't a public display; our picnic table had been strategically positioned behind a bush so that we could be heard but not seen by the other guests, taking their aperitif on the terrace. M. le Comte had the consideration to appear from behind the bush carrying an ice bucket and two glasses of champagne, and thus sozzled we felt no need to move until the hooting of owls close at hand scared the children off the lawn.

The following day, armed with the Count's instructions

on how to avoid the holiday traffic, we set a course for the home of a Viscount, on the Normandy coast near St Malo.

Vicomte Fou de Kerdaniel turned out to be a small, terrier-like man who looked rather like a French Colombo but without the raincoat. His Château de Bonabry was a clutch of handsomely decaying 16th century buildings gathered around a courtyard full of sleeping dogs. There were several horses in the stable, and an old Citroen van for the dogs' overnight accommodation. Hunting was the Kerdaniel passion.

The Vicomtesse had a certain air of refinement, but it was the Vicomte who was descended from 500 years of Fou de Kerdaniels. He had been born, educated (by a priest), and married (presumably also by a priest) in the Château, and as it wasn't possible to secure such a large building against burglars, he also stayed here all year round to defend it.

Happily he wasn't in the least bit bothered by the children's lack of etiquette, although when I turned up in a jacket for dinner, he nipped upstairs and put one on too, to make me feel at ease. How did the British aristocracy survive, he wanted to know. Did they also do B&B?

Of the three guest rooms, ours was the pink suite, all escritoires, canopied beds, paintings of ancestors, parquet flooring that smelled of linseed oil, and windows that looked out over a walled garden of lawn, dahlias and tomato beds.

Various paths headed off through the château woodlands towards the beach at Bonabry, which dissolved into the distance just like those watercolours of northern France that grace my parents' sitting room. In fact the sea retreated so far - four kilometres - that it was only with the aid of the occasional very distant basket-carrying shellfish-gatherer that we could be sure where the heat haze ended and the water began.

We spent a couple of happy days here, meandering down through the grounds to the beach, and wandering out to find the tide. The Vicomtesse introduced the children to a set of terrier puppies living in the stables, and after that it was hard to lure them away even with bucket and spade.

"Don't turn it into a hotel", I said when the time came for us to go. And as the gravel crunched under our wheels, the Vicomte agreed that he never would.

Richard Binns

A Run to the Sun

Fast "Runs to the Sun" across France have two major drawbacks. First, if you use only toll autoroutes from Calais to the Mediterranean you will be £40 out of pocket before you even catch sight of its azure waters. Second, if you drive exclusively on routes nationales and D roads you must take care to respect all French speed limits, especially in built-up areas; on-the-spot fines are draconian - minimum 100-150 euros.

My 650-mile long sun run is an ideal compromise and offers four benefits: you'll not pay one euro in tolls; two-thirds of the run is on toll-free autoroutes (part of the A16, A28, A75) and motorway-standard dual carriageways; the route avoids all city and large town centres; and no other toll-free run gets you to the Med so quickly. (You can cheat a little and pay tolls on the A16/A77/ A719/A71.)

I've provided details of 36 hotels and restaurants on the run and I've given them all cooking ratings (1-5; basic to superb); three in each of the three parts are, for varying reasons, particular favourites of mine (marked *). For those of you who like a break or the idea of a lazy run south, I've highlighted 30 scenic detours.

French driving musts

1. Observe speed limits. Built-up areas 50kph (31mph): town or village name starts the limit; bar through name is the derestriction sign. Ordinary roads 90kph (56mph): if wet

80kph (50mph). Toll-free autoroutes and dual carriageways 110kph (68mph); if wet 100kph (62mph). Other autoroutes 130kph (81mph); if wet 110kph (68mph).

2. Do not drink and drive. The alcohol limit is lower in France than Britain: 50mg per 100ml of blood: for men the equivalent of one pint of beer; for women, half a pint. Fines can be as high as 5000 euros.

3. Belt up (front/rear); seat under-10s in the back.

4. Take a full set of spare bulbs for the car.

5. Take a red warning triangle for any breakdowns.

6. Take a spiral-bound Michelin atlas.

7. Buy fuel at supermarkets for big savings.

Part One

The route Calais to Chartres 221 miles.
Calais. A16. Boulogne bypass (N1). (Do not use A16 from Boulogne to Abbeville as this section is a toll autoroute; though I think I would cheat and pay up!) N1. Abbeville bypass (A28). A28. N28. Approaching Rouen the A28/N28 descends steeply towards the Seine; first through a mile-long tunnel, then under a railway bridge and next a short tunnel. Before this short tunnel keep right and follow signs for Vernon/Pontoise; at the traffic lights turn left and follow signs for Vernon/Evreux. N15 (some useful recent improvements). N154. Evreux bypass (recently extended 10 miles to south). N154. N12. Dreux bypass. N154 (this is almost all dual carriageway now). Chartres bypass (N123).

WHERE TO STAY

1)   Liégeoise et Atlantic Hôtel: 62930 Wimereux (03 21

32 41 01). Cooking 2-3. Very comfortable restaurant with rooms. First floor salle beside the sea. Lift. English-speaking owners, Alain and Béatrice Delpierre. He tackles classical and modern courses. Super fish plats.

2) Métropole: 51 r. Thiers, 62200 Boulogne-sur-Mer (03 21 31 54 30). Comfortable hotel (no restaurant). Spacious bedrooms. Lift. Garden. Garage.

3) Matelote: 80 bd Ste-Beuve, 62200 Boulogne-sur-Mer (03 21 30 17 97). Cooking 3. Very comfortable restaurant. Classical and neo-classical fish repertoire from Tony Lestienne. Wife Régine is a much liked patronne. (Note: rooms now available.)

4) Restaurant de Nausicaa: bd Ste-Beuve, 62200 Boulogne-sur-Mer (03 21 33 24 24). Cooking 1-2. Comfortable restaurant supervised by Tony Lestienne (see above, where rooms now available). Classical fish dishes dominate.

5) Host. de la Rivière: 62360 Pont-de-Briques (03 21 32 22 81). Cooking 3. Very comfortable restaurant with rooms. Garden. Elegant dining room. Lovely owners Jean and Odette Martin. Classical/regional plats, mainly fish-based.

6) *Aub. La Grenouillière: 62170 Madelaine-sous-Montreuil (03 21 06 07 22). Cooking 3-4. comfortable restaurant with rooms. Quiet. Garden. Cottages beside tree-lined stream. Enjoy Roland Gauthier's neo-classical/modern repertoire.

7) *Château de Montreuil: 62170 Montreuil (03 21 81 53 04). Cooking 3-4. Very comfortable hotel. Quiet. Large garden. Patronne Lindsay Germain is an English rose; chef/husband Christian cooks neo-classical/modern gems.

8) Aub. Le Fiacre: 80120 Quend (03 22 23 47 30). Cooking 1-2. Comfortable restaurant with rooms. Quiet. Gardens. Half-timbered farm houses restaurant; modern

annexe at rear. Classical dishes.

9) Aub. du Beau Lieu: rte Gournay, 76440 Forges-les-Eaux (02 35 90 50 36). Cooking 2-3. Comfortable restaurant with rooms. Marie-France Ramelet is proud of her cave (40 halves) and beamed salle. Chef Patrick is a modern master.

10) Paix: 15 r. Neufchâtel, 76440 Forges-les-Eaux (02 35 90 51 22). Cooking 1-2. Simple hotel. Garden. Parking. Much-liked Régine and Rémy Michel are Normandy cooking addicts. Spanking new bedrooms and lift.

11) *Chaîne d'Or: 27700 Les Andelys (02 32 54 00 31). Cooking 3. Very comfortable rest, with rooms. Quiet. Beside Seine. Impeccably run by Monique and Carole Foucault. The chef is much praised.

12) France: 29 r. St-Thomas, 27000 Evreux (02 32 39 09 25). Cooking 2-3. Very comfortable restaurant with rooms. Quietish street 500m north of cathedral. Easy access from north. Neo-classical/classical dishes.

Scenic Breaks

A. Côte d'Opale: The coast north of Boulogne is renowned for sandy beaches, dunes, cliffs and the invigorating Channel views from Cap Gris-Nez and Cap Blanc-Nez. For longer breaks hire bikes from cycle shops at Wissant and Wimille.

B. Course Valley: Minutes from the N1 but what a contrast. The D127 is especially delightful between Inxent (admire the old auberge), Beussent and Doudeauville (enjoy a drink on the grassy bank opposite the Café des Sports).

C. Montreuil: Once a Roman port, the hilltop town is now 10km inland. Enter through the northern medieval porte, explore the huge place, wander the cobbled streets and walk the 3km circuit of the Vauban-designed ramparts.

D. Crécy: Here Edward III won his famous 1346 victory, the start of the 100 Years War. From a viewing tower survey the battlefield where, for the first and not the last time, such stunning use was made of the longbow.

E. Marquenterre: Explore the 370-acre Parc Ornithologique. The "sea which enters the land" is a mix of marshes, dunes and salt pastures and is renowned for migrating birds. Details from the Domaine at St-Quentin-en-Tourmont.

F. Rambures: There's nothing prissy about the virile château; the 15th-century castle has thick-walled, red-brick towers, topped with cone-shaped roofs. Rambures played an important part in the 100 Years war. (Closed Wednesday.)

G. Forêt d'Eu: An exhilarating beech forest. Visit the viewpoint at the Poteau de Ste-Catherine; and the tiny War Graves (Commonwealth) Cemetery at Grandcourt, the last resting place for 58 souls (study the register, map and table).

H. Forges-les-Eaux: An unassuming one-time spa: a combination of woods, lake, park and varied leisure activities. The casino will attract some; for others the Resistance Museum will be more interesting (pm only).

I. Les Andelys: The ruins of the fortress, the once mighty Château Gaillard, built by Richard the Lionheart in 1196, dominates the town and the Seine. Alas, the redoubtable castle was captured by the French seven years later.

J. Maintenon: The 500 year-old Renaissance château is constructed from grey and pink stone and brickwork and has different shaped towers and turrets. The exterior is complemented by water features and a Le Notre-designed park.

Part Two

The route Chartres to Clermont-Ferrand 239 miles.
N154. N20. Approaching Orléans, pass under the N60 road bridge (the northern bypass) and then immediately right, following signs for Montargis. N60. D952. Gien. D952. N7 (Toll A77 available). Nevers bypass. N1. Moulins bypass. N7. D46. St-Pourçain. N9. Gannat. (Toll A719/A71 available.) N9. Riom bypass.

Where to stay

1) Novotel: 28000 Chartres (02 37 88 13 50). Cooking 1. Very comfortable hotel. Swimming pool. Gardens. Lift. Just west of the A10 exit 2. Basic cooking. 78 rooms. Open all year. All cards.

2) Ibis: 28110 Luce (Chartres suburb) (02 37 35 76 00). Cooking 1. Simple hotel. Easy to find: just east of N123 Chartres bypass and N23 intersection. Basic fare. 74 rooms. Open all year. All cards.

3) Orléans Parc Hôtel: 45380 La Chapelle-St-Mesmin (Orléans) (02 38 43 26 26). Cooking 2. Comfortable hotel. Quiet. Beside Loire. Park. From N20 use N60 (Orléans bypass); alongside N152 and just west of A71. Neo-classical cuisine.

4) *Aub. des Templiers: 45290 Boismorand (Les Bézards) (02 38 31 80 01). Cooking 3-4. Luxury hotel; one of France's finest. Large park. Pool. Tennis.

5) Rivage: 45500 Gien (02 38 37 79 00). Cooking 3 (often 2). Very comfortable hotel, overlooking Loire. Parking. Modern/neo-classical plats.

6) Lion d'Or: 18240 Léré (02 48 72 60 12). Cooking 2.

Comfortable restaurant with rooms. Village on Loire's west bank. Neo-classical and classical fare.

7) *Coq Hardi et Hôtel Relais Fleuri: 58150 Pouilly-sur-Loire (03 86 39 12 99). Cooking 2. Comfortable restaurant with rooms. Near Loire. English-speaking hosts, Philippe and Dominique Martin. Classical cooking. 9 rooms. Closed 1 Dec-20 Jan. Tuesday evening and Wednesdays (October-April). All cards.

8) Grand Monarque: 58400 La Charité-sur-Loire (03 86 70 21 73). Cooking 2 (sometimes 1). Comfortable hotel. Overlooking Loire. Garden.

9) *Renaissance: 58470 Magny-Cours (03 86 58 10 40). Cooking 3. Very comfortable restaurant with rooms. Quiet. Classical/neo-classical twists and turns.

10) Paris-Jacquemart: 21 r. Paris, 03000 Moulins (04 70 44 00 58). Cooking 3. Very comfortable hotel. Lift. Pool. Louis and Anne-Françoise de Roberty have restored pride to this once famed hotel. Neo-classical cooking.

11) Aub. de la l'Orisse: 03150 Varennes-sur-Allier (04 70 45 05 60). Cooking 1. Comfortable hotel. Pool. Tennis. Logis in large grounds, south of town (at N7/N209 junc.). New owners.

12) Chêne Vert: 03500 St-Pourçain-sur-Sioule (04 70 45 40 65). Cooking 2-3. Comfortable hotel. Parking. Jean-Guy and Martine Siret have brightened up the hotel no end. Enjoy both his neo-classical fare and the local wines.

SCENIC BREAKS

A. Chartres: The wondrous cathedral, with gigantic twin towers, is first spotted from miles away. Relish the fine carvings and the medieval stained glass windows. Explore, too, old Chartres to the east.

B. Parc Floral (Orléans): At Olivet, south of the Loire. From April to October there's always a colourful show of flowers and shrubs in the 74-acre park.

C. St-Benoît-sur-Loire/Germigny-des-Prés:Two ecclesiastical treasures. The Romanesque basilica at St-Benoît where the belfry porch is majestic. The tiny mosaic roof in the small church at Germigny is a rare jewel.

D. Forêt d'Orléans: The vast broad-leaved forest is at its most alluring between Sully and Lorris. Seek out the moving, sequoia-shaded Lorris maquis memorial at the Carrefour de la Résistance.

E. St-Fargeau: In the Puisaye, famed for its stoneware (from red and white clay seams). The huge château has several ugly towers and a gorgeous interior courtyard. Children will love the nearby Ferme du Château.

F. Pouilly-sur-Loire: A 30-second detour to Les Berthiers, east of the N7 and 2km north of Pouilly. At the Domaine Landrot-Guyollot an exceptional daughter and father duo, English-speaking Sophie and René, make super wines.

G. La Charité-sur-Loire: Visit the Eglise Notre-Dame. The vast Romanesque wonder is noted for its chevet, domed transept, handsome choir and radiating chapels, and the Max Ingrand stained-glass windows.

H. Apremont-sur-Allier: The unspoilt, picturesque riverside setting has a wide grass walkway, shaded by willows and a line of brown-shuttered, ivy-covered houses. Flower-filled village. Visit the pretty Parc Floral (closed Tues).

I. Souvigny: West of the River Allier and Moulins (smile at the latter's Jacquemart clock tower) and the Priory of St-Pierre with its 12th century calendrier, a carved octagonal stone pillar showing scenes from the Zodiac.

J. Vichy: Described by wine merchant Robin Yapp as "caught in a fin de siècle time-warp". Riverside park, the Parcs d'Allier; a Parc des Sources with covered galleries; a casino and several other late 19th century buildings.

Part Three

The route Clermont Ferrand to Clermont-l'Hérault 190 miles.

To avoid tolls do not join A71 at junction 13 (east of Riom). Instead continue south on Riom bypass (D447) and N9 for 8 1/2 miles (from start of Riom bypass) to island with traffic lights where follow signs east for A71/A710/A72/A75 Lyon/Montpellier. Join A71/A75 at junction 15. A75. N9. Millau bypass. N9. A75 to junction with N9/N109 north of Clermont-l'Hérault.

WHERE TO STAY

1) *Rose des Vents: 63530 Volvic (04 73 33 50 77). Cooking 2. Comfortable hotel. Quiet. Pool. Tennis. Lift. Gardens. Marvellous setting, 2,500ft high in Volcans parc naturel. Easily reached from N9. Classical cooking flows.

2) Chalut: 63490 Sauxillanges (04 73 96 80 71). Cooking 2. Simple restaurant with basic rooms. Garage. François Chalut's neo-classical/regional menus include a five course dessert version, ideal for sweet-toothers.

3) Poste et Champanne: 43100 Brioude (04 71 50 14 62). Cooking 1-2. Simple hotel. Parking. The town's new bypass means Brioude is now much quieter. Book an annexe room. Regional/classical repertoire.

4) Grand Hôtel Voyageurs: 25 r. Collège, 15100 St-Flour (04 71 60 34 44). Cooking 2. Comfortable hotel. Garage. Lift. In the haute ville with delectable sun-trap terrace (alas not used for meals). Neo-classical/regional dishes.

5) Rocher Blanc: La Garde, 48200 Albaret-Ste-Marie (04 66 31 90 09). Cooking 1. Simple hotel, 3,000ft high, 2km north of A75 exit 32. Pool. Garden. The Brunels provide wide choice classical/regional/Bourgeoise grub.

6) Grand Hôtel Prouhèze: 48130 Aumont-Aubrac (04 66 42 80 07). Cooking 3. Comfortable family hotel. Guy Prouhèze is the 4th generation chef; classical/regional dishes. Wife Catherine is an extrovert hostess.

7) Capelle: 7 r. Fraternité, 12100 Millau (05 65 60 14 72). Simple hotel (no restaurant). Quiet. Owner Jane Roquet is a delight. Park in the large place opposite the hotel. Short walk to Capion restaurant (see below).

8) Capion: 3 r. J.-F. Alméras, 12100 Millau (05 65 60 00 91). Cooking 1-2. Simple restaurant. No prizes for the décor but Patrick Mougeot's classical/neo-classical/regional plats should please all.

9) Château de Creissels: rte St-Affrique (D992), 12100 Millau (05 65 60 16 59). Cooking 2 (often 1). Comfortable hotel. Quiet. Garden. Well appointed bedrooms; public rooms have old-world gentility. Regional/classical dishes.

10) *Midi-Papillon: 12230 St-Jean-du-Bruel (05 65 62 26 04). Cooking 2. Simple hotel. Quiet. Pool. Worth the detour. Maryse and Jean-Michel Papillon are involved 4th generation owners. He cooks all styles of plats.

11) *Mimosa: 34725 St-Guiraud (04 67 96 67 96). What a superb finale for the Sun Run: GO! Cooking 3-4. Comfortable restaurant Bridget Pugh's inventive cooking is full of harmonious, natural flavours. Rooms? See next entry.

12) Ostalario Cardabela: 34725 St-Saturnin-de-Lucian (04 67 88 62 62). Simple hotel. Pughs' annexe is 11/2 miles north of Mimosa; transport laid on if required. Old house with stylishly decorated and furnished rooms.

SCENIC BREAKS

A. Usson: Drive up to the village, east of Issoire, and then climb to the Statue de la Vierge on a basalt peak with extensive views.

B. Brioude: The marvellous Basilica of St-Julien, hemmed in by buildings, has dozens of shades and types of patterned and layered stones.

C. St-Flour: A strategically important site, especially during the Hundred Years War. The town sits atop an impressive 100m-high basalt table.

D. Château d'Alleuze/Viaduc-de-Garabit: The eerie ruins of the castle, on a rocky pyramid, compares starkly with two other nearby man-made modern marvels: the massive railway viaduct built by Eiffel; and the gigantic A75 viaduct.

E. Gorges du Tarn: A spectacular scenic thrill. Head downstream from Ste-Enimie to Le Rozier: the combination of extensive woods on the steep sides of the gorge, topped by rock sculptures, and the emerald Tarn water is enthralling.

F. Chaos de Montpellier-le-Vieux: North-east of Millau, a collection of weirdly shaped, fancifully named rocks litter the limestone causse (plateau).

G. Roquefort-sur-Soulzon: Home of the king of cheeses. Visit, free of charge, the caves which are the world's best natural refrigerators. Here blue-veined ewes' milk cheeses mature into the unique Roquefort taste.

H. La Couvertoirade: The tiny, fortified hamlet, once a

Templar staging post, features stone used in many ways: note the roof tiles (lauzes).

I.   Le Caylar: The village (caylar: rock) sits under a pyramid of oddly shaped rocks. Admire the eye-catching dead elm tree sculptured by Michel Chevray.

J.   Grotte de Clamouse: Caves as good as any in France. A one km guided tour (English notes available) winds through wonderfully lit passages and vast caverns with tens of thousands of fascinating formations.

Article References

La Chateau de la Commanderie

Farges-Allichamps, 18200 St Amand - Montrond
Tel: 02.48.61.04.19 Fax: 02.48.61.01.84
Email: commanderie@ila-chateau.com
Website: ila-chateau.com/command/

ot-nuits-st-georges.fr

Official website of Nuits-St-Georges where Justine Hardy stayed.
Includes town maps, contact details of restaurants and hotels, an
events calendar and area guide.

General Web Resources

francetourism.com/driving_france.asp

Extensive information site on all aspects of driving in France
including tolls, insurance, maps, licences, services, hitch-hiking,
the French highway code, and regional information centres.

budgettravel.com/euroroad.htm

Not a particularly attractive site, but this is a good source of links
and further resources to help you plan your drive.

day-tripper.net

Another garish site for the cross-channel tripper, but with some
useful information on the autoroute network, tips for driving in
France, locations of garages, distances between towns, and
insurance requirements.

autoroutes.fr

Information, in both French and English, on tolls, mileage between given destinations, restaurants, service stations and hotels along the way. More than 13 million routes and itineraries available.

mappy.com
Great website, easy to use and available in lots of different languages, providing routes and itineraries from A-B all over Europe in good detail, giving journey times and tolls (or routes avoiding them). Also has detailed town maps showing car parks and petrol stations, up-to-date weather information and ideas for hotels and accommodation, and entertainment.

viamichelin.com
Online site of the famous Michelin driving guides with directions, maps and so on.

Autoroute information
For motorway conditions in France call +33 (0)1 4705 9001

Drive Holiday Specialists

Motours
Self drive summer holidays to France & nine other European countries. Hotels, villas, holiday villages, theme parks, camping and mobile homes. Tel: 01892 677777; web: motours.co.uk

Becks Holidays in France
This company has 20 year's experience organising self-drive, self-catering holidays for all ages on campsites with comfortable mobile homes and good facilities for children. Tel: 01273 842843

Drive Alive
Aims to offer holidays in Europe for motorists at unbeatable value. Website (drive-alive.co.uk) covers all aspects of driving holidays including channel crossings, breakdown, insurance, hotels, tolls, maps and useful links. Tel: 0870 745 7979.

Driveline

Online operator organising self-drive breaks, offering deals with Eurostar & Hoverspeed. Tel: 0870 756 7564. See driveline.co.uk.

Castle and Chateaux Resources

Relais et Chateaux

This well established guide to smart hotels in France - many of them chateaux - uses five criteria to measure its carefully chosen properties; courtesy, charm, character, calm and cuisine. See relaischateaux.com.

Chateaux France

Listing chateaux, manors, abbeys, fortresses and luxury private mansions in towns and villages. Also suggests restaurants and historical visits. See chateaux-france.com

Chateaux et Hotels

Chain offering 532 'charming castles', guesthouses and romantic hotels throughout France. Also makes a selection of 121 traditional gourmet restaurants. chateauxethotels.com

Castles of France

Site of French 'artist photographer' Georges d'Alba - a somewhat home-made affair for castle groupies, with more than 500 photos of castles, abbeys, churches, fortresses and keeps. D'Alba also welcomes guests to his own castle. See castles-france.net

Recommended Reading

France on Backroads:
The Motorist's Guide to the French Countryside.
Duncan-Petersen/Hunter Publishing. ISBN: 1556507755

France Road Atlas Michelin Travel. ISBN: 2060002672

Frommer's France's Best-Loved Driving Tours: 25 Unforgettable Itineraries. ISBN: 0028638387

Driving Tours France - Automobile Association. Macmillan. ISBN: 0028604512

On the Road Around Normandy, Brittany and the Loire Valley : Driving Holidays in Northern France by Roger Thomas, Lucy Koserski (Editor). Passport Books. ISBN: 0844290114

On the Road Around the South of France : France's Mediterranean Coast, Province, the Cote D'Azur, Coastal Languedoc and the Auvergne by Nick Hanna, Melissa Shales (Editor). Passport Books. ISBN: 0844249548

France by Auto: A Practical Man's Guide to Adventures in France by John A. Hale. Hats Off Books. ISBN: 1587360039

France: Charming Inns and Itineraries by Karen Brown; see also karenbrown.com/franceinns/itinerary.html

Hotels and Country Inns of Character and Charm in France Hunter Publishing; ISBN 2743607408

THINGS TO DO 'BEFORE YOU DIE' No. 744

Bike Bordeaux and Burgundy
"Hell, one deserves a little comfort now and then. So for a special occasion, book the ultra-sybaritic Butterfield & Robinson biking trip to Bordeaux and Burgundy. During the day, you'll be biking on relatively flat terrain, stopping for private wine tastings at such famous vineyards as Mouton-Rothschild and Chambolle Musigny. At night, you'll be staying at 16th and 17th century chateaux where dinner is a gluttonous feast, washed down by, what else, more excellent wine." *Steve Jermanok*

Activity France

Activity France

Just as France is blessed with a wide variety of fresh produce, enabling it to have developed the most sophisticated cuisine in the Western world, so the range of landscapes and geological conditions make France an excellent destination for activity holidays. France has that heady mix of landscape and climate and comfort which means that canoeing on a French river can double as a sunbathing holiday in summer, or walking amongst Bordeaux vineyards a gastronomic adventure as well as an attempt to keep fit.

Recent years have seen an explosion in activity holiday companies, and the development of the internet has allowed even those at the local level to reach a wide audience. For it is these smaller outfits who often provide the best value and the keenest knowledge of local conditions. Moreover, the influx of Northern Europeans into rural France, especially the British, Dutch and Germans, seeking a 'better life' at favourable prices, has also led to a growth in 'ex-pat' industries - and many of these revolve around tourism.

But bear in mind that personal recommendation and referral at this level is extremely important, as the internet can allow all sorts of people to market sub-standard packages.

Below we have included three features by TI writers who

specialise in activities. Alf Alderson writes extensively on mountains, biking and hiking, and Christopher Somerville's Walks of the Month are a familiar feature to Sunday Telegraph readers.

The Planning section is correspondingly longer than others in the book because of the wealth of companies, both small and large, who are operating in France. As well as the reputable market leaders we have included a mix of smaller specialists to inspire you to research a little further. Not least because in doing so you will discover what a wealth of activity options there are in France.

Andrew Eames

CANOEING THE CHARENTE RIVER

Somewhere just west of Jarnac, southwest France, Thomas (aged four) and I came up with a new song. It was sung to the tune of "She'll be coming round the Mountain", with lyrics that had been specially created for the occasion:

"We're coming down the river in a boat" (Thomas: "in a boat")

"We're coming down the river in a boat" (Thomas: "in a boat")

"We're coming down the river, coming down the river",

"Coming down the river in a boat" (Thomas: "in a boat").

On the riverbank, an old fisherman and his wife peered at us through thick glasses from behind a trestle table groaning with a lavish Sunday lunch. "Il est content" - he's happy - I heard the old bloke say as we drifted past. Could he mean me?

It was intended to be an old-fashioned, "Swallows and Amazons" sort of holiday, just me and my boy, a Canadian canoe, a tent, and a placid French river brimming with fish. I am delighted to say that, despite the potential for disaster, that was how it turned out. Dappled mornings, tumbling weirs, and lashings of fresh air.

The Charente flows through southwest France, rising near Limoges and making its bow into the curtains of the Atlantic near La Rochelle. Somewhere in the middle it meanders through the vineyards of Cognac country, which is where this journey began.

Getting a four-year-old native of West London into an open canoe, sleeping under the stars and eating funny foreign food, is a piece of cake - provided it's attractively sandwiched within return journeys on the Eurostar and the TGV. The concept of a river voyage didn't really begin to strike home until we'd been afloat for an hour, and Thomas decided it was time we went back.

"Back" was Les Gabariers, a riverside bar southwest of Angouleme owned by an Englishman, Simon Constant. Constant has been arranging canoe hire from here for some years, and there's an air of the "Wind in the Willows" about the place, expressed by a variety of rivercraft in varying states of decay, dogs, ducks and swans, and a collection of venerable mopeds outside the bar suggesting that the denizens of the riverbank are within.

My mid-river revelation that we were not going back to Gabariers for three whole days produced a torrent of "whys" from Thomas. It took a whole new made-up story about a frog that decided to go on holiday to distract him. That's one advantage of going downstream; you can ship paddles and do your story telling with no fear that the scenery will begin to rewind.

By lunchtime he was absorbed in the journey. We stopped to heat up some baked beans - mon dieu, la gastronomie anglaise - on the river bank, and then drifted with a fishing rod made from a stick, trying to attract perch with pungent maturing frankfurters.

By mid afternoon the sun was showing no mercy so we struck off up a narrow, fast-flowing cut, which broadened into a mill pool surrounded by decaying mill buildings in lichen-coated limestone. This was Vibrac, where I knew there was a bar called Coco's.

There were four mopeds outside Coco's, and four pastis-drinking paysans inside. "Coca-Cola!?" repeated the lady proprietor, as if we'd asked for Ecstasy. They had none, never had, and I suspect never will. On the wall were dog-eared black and white photos of Vibrac as it used to be; absolutely nothing had changed. What was wrong with these people? Hadn't they heard of downshifting or teleworking?

We stopped for the night opposite St.Simon, pitching our tent amidst the trees amongst undergrowth that smelled of mint.

Next morning I woke to a sound which I had hoped not to hear: the patter of rain. For some while we lay cosily in our sleeping bags and watched it fall, but it showed no sign of relenting. A quick phone call to the local taxi company, and half an hour later we were in a trendy bar in Jarnac, watching rock videos.

The next day's weather was kinder. We had a lovely passage, ticking off the romanesque churches and family-owned cognac distilleries as they drifted astern. At midday we completed what became known as the two ice-cream walk; I wanted to see the 13th century Benedictine abbey at Bassac, but incentives were required to get Thomas the mile uphill from the river.

"The Sisters of Ursula welcome Visitors", said a notice outside the abbey church. I wasn't sure the Sisters of Ursula would welcome a four-year-old in wellies and singlet and carrying a Kermit the Frog ice cream. Especially as there were holy noises emanating from behind the abbey church door.

By the early afternoon we were nearing Jarnac, and I was listening to cricket on my short-wave radio while quaffing red wine and Hula Hoops. At the lock above the town we had a stroke of good fortune: a hire boat full of jolly Germans was coming upstream, and they did all the hard work with the gates and winches.

At Jarnac itself there was a lock-keeper on duty, and we sat alone in the middle of the huge, emptying bath, father and son dwindling downwards as the prison walls grew higher, watched by groups of curious, pointing tourists.

We didn't stop at Jarnac, having seen it all before. It was the weekend, and suddenly the river seemed almost crowded. Cries of "cochon" went up from the riverbank at every hint of motorboat wash. Not only had these people not heard of teleworking, their cursing was old-fashioned too.

That evening we came ashore for the last time at Bourg Charente, made the required phone call, and lay down on the grassy banks to wait for Simon to come with his trailer to take father and son back to the world of the TGV, work and school.

Alf Alderson

There are some times when I'm walking or mountain biking in the mountains that I feel quite churlish. These instances occur when I meet another walker or biker coming in the opposite direction.

You know how it is - you feel compelled to be the cheery hiker/biker, to hail your fellow traveller with a hearty "Hello!"; maybe even a quick comment on how wonderful the scenery, the trail, the weather is.

Yet what I really want is to maintain the solitude of being alone in the hills, for in many ways that's what is so special about wild country. And when someone who has just as much right as me to be in that same wild landscape crosses my path it kind of spoils it for me (and who knows, maybe I spoil it for them too...).

So when I had the chance to go back to the St. Engrace Valley in the Pyrenees Atlantiques last May, I knew that my involuntary churlishness wouldn't be a problem. This is a part of the Pyrenees that sees few visitors despite its undoubted loveliness - and please don't all rush there at once now I've said that; the ever-present paradox of travel writing is that as soon as you describe a beautiful place to others you run the risk of destroying the very thing you're writing about.

But let's take that risk. For I don't imagine the St. Engrace valley will ever get too crowded - it just seems to get passed by for the higher and more dramatic mountain scenery to the east.

That said, snow-topped peaks of more than 6,000 feet look down on the valley, beneath which are dark green pine forests and emerald green alpine pastures, whilst down in the valley bottom, clinging to the steep hillsides, lie small hamlets and the handsome Basque farmhouses so characteristic of this area.

The most remarkable features of the valley are the huge limestone gorges slicing into its southern slopes. The Gorges de Kakoueta and its smaller companion the Gorges d'Ehujarrem, rarely visited by tourists, are amongst the deepest limestone gorges in Europe; massive slashes in the landscape created through the action of rainwater and gradual uplift of the valley over aeons.

Looking across to the gorges from the northern slopes of the valley you can see how even now their headwalls are being eaten back, nibbling into the mountains above them and inexorably burrowing towards the Spanish border running along the mountain tops.

If you take the time to walk or mountain bike up the hillsides on either side of the Gorges de Kakoueta the view down into the deep, dank bottom of the canyon almost induces vertigo - you begin to understand where the urge to throw yourself off a high place comes from - and if you wander into the bottom of the gorge you enter a world about as far removed from the air and light of the mountains above as can be imagined.

There are places down here where the sun never shines, and exotic and prehistoric-looking ferns drape themselves down the canyon walls in an environment that is forever damp.

Beneath the gorges are some of the deepest and longest subterranean passageways in Europe, obviously popular with cavers, although the attraction of this sport has always been lost on me - why go to the bright, sunlit heights of the Pyrenees to then scurry underground into utter blackness for the day?

Even the gorges, spectacular though they are, don't hold the attraction of the mountains and valleys of the area. The rich greens of the landscape, the brightness of the high level snows, and the ever-changing light (and weather) make for an exhilarating environment to explore by foot and bike. On a bike you can enjoy the landscape off road or on - occasionally the Tour de France passes through the area, and you can test yourself on mountain passes such as the Port de Larrau which has been used in the Tour in the past. Unlike the riders you can enjoy the luxury of looking out across much of southwest France and north east Spain when you eventually reach the summit.

On my first visit to the St. Engrace area two years ago I saw four hikers and one mountain biker on the area's numerous trails and footpaths - in three weeks. Last May I was there for a couple of days (staying at the friendly gîte d'etape at St.Engrace hamlet, opposite the imposing 11th century church) when I met just two walkers following the GR10 route from the Atlantic coast to the Mediterranean, so things still don't seem to be too hectic in the area.

Perhaps it will always remain that way. The area isn't pushed too fiercely by the tourist board or the locals, and whether that's a conscious decision or not I certainly applaud it - hidden gems such as this are harder and harder to find these days, which makes them all the more valuable when you do stumble across them.

Christopher Somerville

The two men had obviously got into the boat with the best of intentions - a sheaf of fishing rods, all set up and ready in the prow, bore witness to that. But the hot sun and the warm thick air of the Marais Poitevin had got to them about the same time as the wine. They lolled shirtless on the thwarts, sound asleep, an empty bottle propped between them, as we sculled quietly by along the sunbaked quays of Coulon.

"Yes," murmured Bertrand the boatman, "the Marais is not for hurrying. Here you have to learn to take things easy."

Soon we turned aside from the main river and slipped under a low bridge into the *conches*, a tangle of weed-carpeted waterways overhung with wetland trees - poplar, alder, willow. The Atlantic coast of France was sweltering on this hot summer's afternoon, but here on the water all was cool and shady. A dense canopy of leaves filtered the sunlight into brilliant bars and pools. Every sound seemed soporific - the clop and swish of Bertrand's oar, the hum of dragonflies, the tearing sound of fat white cattle chomping grass in the marsh meadows. For all I cared, lounging back in sunhat and shirtsleeves, the boat might creep on like this for ever, deeper and deeper into the wet green ways of the La Venise Verte, the Green Venice of the marshes.

Coulon, 25 miles inland as the heron flies, is the capital of the marais mouilles (wet marshes), one of two very distinctive landscapes that together make up the 200,000-

acre triangular tableland known as the Marais Poitevin. The triangle lies on its side, its base facing west to the Atlantic coast, its apex pointing a little east of Coulon. Inland it is mostly marais mouilles, lushly green, thick with trees, veined with conches, flooded every winter. Further west the marais desseches (dried marshes) spread out, a great prairie of drained arable land where villages ride every slight rise in the ground.

"You have to try and imagine two thousand years ago," said Bertrand, steering on through shadow and sunlight, "when there was no Marais Poitevin. Where we are boating now would have been under the sea, but already silting up fast. By the time the monks started reclaiming the land, the whole area was one enormous swamp dotted with little islands."

The marais mouilles stayed a flood-ridden swamp until Napoleonic times, when the conches were dug to drain off at least some of the water. A watery way of life developed here, and still persists. Fragile looking boats with pointed prows are still the main means of transport in a place where there are far more watercourses than roads. Loads of hay, cattle, horses, groceries, children on their way to school, curious tourists; everything and everyone goes by water in the marais mouilles.

Along the main river, the Sevres-Niortaise, I had noticed the big flat plate boats moored under the weeping willows, so laden with hay that their hulls were invisible. Now among the tree-hung side channels we began to meet the smaller sharp-prowed yoles *(light boats)* carrying farmers to and from their pasturage fields. A black yole overtook us, an Alsatian dog sitting with ears cocked opposite his master. The man leaned across casually as he passed and shook Bertrand's hand with a muttered "Eanne baɪade - have a good cruise."

The marais mouilles are mainly a summer cruising ground these days, their hinterland growing wild. In winter, rainwater pours off the surrounding uplands into the basin of the Marais Poitevin, once a huge bay of the sea. Medieval monks reclaimed the land for agriculture, but it took the engineering genius of Dutch experts in the 16th century to channel off the floodwater from the hills. The marais mouilles soak it up like a green sponge until every waterway brims over. Then everything floods, and the villages on their humps of ground become island settlements once more.

Towards evening we oared gently back towards Coulon. Under the carpet of duckweed, bubbles of marsh gas moved like fish. Bertrand stirred up the bottom of the conche with his paddle, and a flick of his cigarette lighter set flames dancing across the water.

That evening in the Auberge de l'Ecluse beside the river I ate marsh food - smoked eels, a subtle green vegetable stew simmered in a stockpot, savoury white haricot beans. Frogs were croaking among the reeds, and a black kite whistled high over the poplars. A load of hay went slowly by on its invisible boat.

"They won't bite," said the fishermen at dusk, down by the water's edge. "But who cares?"

Next day I took the romantically named Routes des Iles and went swooping seawards through the grand prairies of the marais desseches. The road dipped and climbed from one former island to the next, each rise of ground straddled by a village. Crossing the boundary between wet and dry marsh, I left the lush tree-lined meadows behind and came into a rich blue and yellow country of lucerne, sunflowers and corn, a painter's landscape. Horizons were far and flat, the enormous skies pierced by church spires, water towers and red-tiled roofs of farm buildings. Every farmhouse had its blue or green shutters, every gatepost its bowl of geraniums.

At Maillezais the Romanesque west front of the church writhed with vigorous carvings: pelicans clutching the heads of peasants, distorted beasts vomiting grinning demons, towers of acrobats. On the outskirts of the village rose the impressive ruins of Maillezais Abbey, shattered by the Wars of Religion that tore France apart in the 16th century.

Maillezais was one of five great abbeys of the Marais, built on the shore of the former Gulf of Poitou, whose monks organised and pushed through the reclamation of the bay. They turned the sea into land, swamp into fertile ground, raw limestone into superbly crafted and decorated buildings. In the ruins lie their simple graves, unmarked by monuments, humble stone-lined coffins just wide enough to hold a human corpse.

I followed the Road of the Isles until it crossed the monks' main drainage channel, the Canal des Cinq Abbés. Then I turned south through big sunflower fields, and came to the mussel-farming port of Charron along side roads lined with tamarisk hedges that were feathering and hissing in a stiff sea wind. What is left of the Bay of Poitou, the Baie de l'Aiguillon, grows mussels in its tidal channels. Here the Atlantic pounds on low cliffs of fractured limestone, and on mudflats and salt marshes. Down at the Port du Pave a brawny freckled mussel fisher, seeing the stranger staring inquisitively at his boat, invited me on board. From a plastic barrel he pulled out ten fathoms of rope thickly encrusted with mussels.

"One year old, and delicious," he said, kissing his

fingertips. "With a little white Pineau, some cream and onions - superbe!"

The church at Esnandes showed another richly carved medieval doorway, and a soaring vaulted interior of bone-white limestone. On the cliffs I bent into the wind and watched elderly fishermen as they perched on spindle-legged platforms above the incoming tide, working a row of ramshackle but effective contraptions. With a tremendous creaking of pulleys and twanging of wires, square nets rose out of the waves bulging with weed and spouting water. Enough small fish were bucketed to make each man's evening meal.

In the morning I found my way to the premises of La Bicyclette Verte. There's nothing like a bicycle for exploring the silent byways of La Venise Verte. That's what I found, pedalling along potholed causeway roads into the heart of the green wilderness. Within half an hour I realised I was comprehensively lost, but with marsh harriers flapping among the poplars and kingfishers arrowing down the duck-weed channels I was content to let chance be the compass bearer .

"To Arcais?" repeated the hay-gatherer I finally came across in a water-girdled meadow. "But all the ways will take you there - eventually. Bonne balade, m'sieur, bonne balade..."

Activity Planning

Travel Specialists

Tall Stories
Runs tailor-made activity trips to France, including 'Multisport Holidays' - based in the Alpine town of Morzine, these offer a variety of different activities: mountain biking, rock climbing, alpine trekking, canyoning, white water rafting or hydrospeeding.
Tel: 01932 252 002; web:tallstories.co.uk

Inntravel
Leading UK activity operator with almost 20 years of experience, Inntravel offers walking, cycling and riding holidays in many regions of France including Provence, Normandy and the Pyrenees. Tel: 01653 629001; web: inntravel.co.uk

Belle France
Specialist in activity holidays in rural France offering walking and cycling tours between hotels and also fixed location stays with self-guided activity options. Tel: 01797 223 777;
web: bellefrance.co.uk

Headwater Holidays
Walking, cycling and canoeing holidays "with major emphasis on off the beaten track destinations, friendly family run hotels and excellent regional cuisine". Tel: (01606) 720033;
web: headwater-holidays.co.uk

Cycling for Softies
Offers self-led, tailor made unescorted biking holidays in beautiful rural areas of France, staying in small family-run hotels.
Tel: 0161 248 8282; web: cycling-for-softies.co.uk

In The Saddle

Specialises in riding holidays around the world. In France they offer a holiday in an old mill near Poitiers with opportunities for riding and cycling. Tel: 01256 851 665; web: inthesaddle.com

French Country Cruises

Navigate yourself around the canals of France in Andrew Brock's traditional Penichettes, ranging from 2 to 12 berth from 18 bases around the country. Tel: 01572 821 330;
web: canals.com/frcntry.htm

France Afloat

Based in France, this company will arrange hire of luxurious canal and river boats from independent boatyards to fit specific holiday requirements. Tel: 01905 616 428; web: franceafloat.com

Local and Web Resources

beyond.fr/sports

A well organised, personal, one-man website with lots of ideas and contact details for adventure activities in the valleys, mountains and villages of Provence. Numerous links to local companies offering ballooning, bungee jumping, cycling, climbing, diving, hang-gliding, hiking, petanque, rafting, sailing, spelunking and windsurfing .

frenchconnections.co.uk/activities/index.html

Less attractive but still useful site with a comprehensive links section for those looking for information and sites for companies specialising in cruising, horseriding, golf, painting, drawing, embroidery, gourmet food and wine, cycling, crafts, carriage driving, climbing, walking, painting, mountain biking, skiing and bridge holidays.

cheval-et-chateaux.com
Organises tours on horseback, bed-and-breakfasting in or near chateaux in the Loire valley.

canals.com
All manner of canal and boating related information, including links to local hire places in France, and the French waterways authority. Functional but fascinating.

Recommended Reading

The Independent Walker's Guide to France
Practical information on 35 walks in 16 of the most beautiful regions in France, by Frank Booth and others. The Independent Walker Series. ISBN: 1566561841

Lonely Planet: Walking in France
Suggested itineraries for scenic walks in 13 regions of France, by Sandra Bardwell and others. Lonely Planet Publications. ISBN: 0864426011

France on Foot: Village to Village, Hotel to Hotel. How to Walk the French Trail System on Your Own Bruce Le Favour, Faith Echtermeyer. Attis Press. ISBN: 0966344804

Cycling in France
18 cycling routes around France, with colour photos and maps. Tim Hughes. The Crowood Press. ISBN: 1861261543

White Water Pyrenees
Information, descriptions and maps of 85 white water rivers in France and Spain. Menasha Ridge Press. ISBN: 0-89732-342-4

Walking in Provence
43 walks in four regions of France - the Alps, Var, Vaucluse and

Provence, by Janette Norton. ISBN: 1852842938

ign.fr
Find maps of all regions of France at the website of the French
National Geographic Institute

Information on the Marais Poitevin

Boat Hire
Trigala (05.49.35.02.29), Place de l'Eglise, Coulon, have
8-seat boats with boatman/guide for hire around the conches of
the marais mouilles .
Self-paddle canoes from Embarcadere Cardinaud, Coulon
(05.49.35.90.47) or Venise Verte Loisirs, Arçais (05 49 35.13.01)

Bicycle Hire
La Bicyclette Verte, rue du Cousault, Arçais (05.49.35.42.56)

Accommodation
Hotel Au Marais, 48, Quai Louis Tardy, Coulon
(05.49.35.90.43). Comfortable small hotel right on the river quay.

Information on Canoeing the Charente

Gabariers Canoeing have all the equipment necessary, including
detailed maps and mountain bikes, and offer a daily pickup
service from selected points on the river, as well as from
Angouleme railway station. A canoe for three days costs c. 30
euros, a tent 28 euros, with a 75 euro deposit. There are several
camp sites along the river, but camping wild is also permissible.
Contact Simon Constant in France on 0033 5 45662311 or in
England on 01295 758282.

Glamour France

Glamour France

Glamour and France can mean many things, from the Crillon on the Place de la Concorde in Paris to the faded glitz of Biarritz. But still, despite its tarnished image, its clogged roads, and the variable quality of its hotel accommodation, the Cote d'Azur remains the destination you'll find more of it than anywhere else in France.

For the magic of the south of France has more to do with an inbuilt sense of superiority than anything, really, to do with money. The climate works, the sea is more sparkling and the people, leavened as they are with the cross-cultural currents of the Mediterranean, have a swagger about them which tells you that Italy cannot be far away.

It was the English who discovered them - touristically speaking. It is no accident that the main seafront strip in Nice is called the *Promenade des Anglais,* nor that the statue that has pride of place a few metres away from the Palais du Festivals in Cannes, where they hold the film festival, is of an english aristocrat who made the place popular. Its heyday was in the 50s and 60s, when old money married Hollywood in the form of Rainier and Grace. Two developments have threatened it since then - the massive explosion of four wheeled transport and the arrival of the low cost airlines into

Nice, which means everyone can now ape the glamour that was for the price of dinner for two in a London restaurant.

Finding it, however, is a different matter altogether. The restaurants and hotels that have sprung up to cater to this mass market have almost ruined the coast for those who care. Yes, there is glamour 'left for tea' as Jim Keeble discovers below, but it is mighty hard to find, and it is here more than anywhere else in France that you have to be careful about where you choose to stay and to eat and to swim and to drive - unless that is, you come with no expectations at all. There are some wonderful restaurants along the coast - small places without telephones and short menus and patrons who don't speak english. Hotels where you will be truly undisturbed, and others where the views and the service and the rooms are breathtaking. And just inland there are a web of hilltop villages which still manage to provide a haven from the madness of the coast.

Glamour is here alright. It's just a matter of finding it.

Jim Keeble

It hadn't started well. As I stepped off the plane at Nice airport I realised I'd left my sunglasses behind. Everyone else put on their shades, a tribe of heliophiles strutting to the terminal, while I stood blinking stupidly in the white Mediterranean sun. I'd come to the Côte d'Azur to be glamorous, and failed at the first hurdle. Being without sunglasses on the Riviera is like forgetting your fork at the Last Supper.

Like most people, I grew up with images of the French Riviera plucked from fairytales - Brigitte Bardot exposing the world's first bikini, Princess Grace being graceful, Mick Jagger strutting his stuff in St.Tropez. Then I lived in Nice for two years in the early 1990s (hey, someone had to) and was bitterly disappointed. In truth, the stretch of coast from Monte Carlo to St.Tropez had little sparkle. Concrete seemed to have spread along the shoreline like algae, and with it crowds, con-men and corruption. There was no magic. No enchantment. Only 1,000 pizza joints selling damp Quattro Stagioni.

My personal disillusion was echoed back in grey London where I read numerous grumblings about the Riviera.

"Today, the Côte d'Azur is Paris without the metro", stated Patrice Miran, a French ecologist. Jeanne Augier, owner of Nice's palatial hotel, the Negresco, declared that the 'Age d'Or' had become the "Age de la Décrépitude". Tourism academic Pierre Gouirand agreed, concluding "The Riviera is now one huge city, 80km long, a French Los Angeles".

I read such quotes with sadness. Surely one of the most beautiful coastlines in the world, the cradle of impressionism and the bikini, couldn't have gone completely to the chiens? Surely some magic, some enchantment survived?

Recently, five years since my last visit, I selflessly decided to return to discover whether there was any glamour left on the Riviera.

Hey. Somebody had to.

First signs, as I blinked like a lost lizard on the tarmac, were not encouraging. Nice airport was thick with planes from Europe's cheapest airlines - Easyjet, Debonair (since defunct), Air Holland, Virgin Express, disgorging herds of spandex-clad visitors into the June swelter. Tourism is booming again on the Côte. Last year nine million tourists spent £2.7 billion there. Which is good for the local economy - not so good for the local glamour.

But I had a plan. As a glamour-gatherer I'd investigate three locations, each one with a celebrity history, each one hidden from the concrete sprawl of the coast. Just six miles from Nice, I arrived at my first; St. Jean Cap-Ferrat, and some of the most expensive real estate in the world.

This narrow peninsula by Villefranche was one of the few places to shine when I lived in Nice. I used to go there to breathe in the scent of orange trees and wealth emanating from behind the high-walled villas. Once the reserve of royalty (King Leopold of Belgium built three mansions here) these pine-fringed palaces were the source of abundant rumours - Mick Jagger had one, as did Liz Taylor, Madonna and U2. The latter was my favourite myth, as I pictured the four members of the band shacked up together like students at university, meeting for cigarettes each morning around the kitchen table.

No-one was ever seen, but the high gates and security cameras of this mini Beverly Hills-sur-Mer invited gossip. After all, isn't that the point of high gates and security cameras?

I headed past the impenetrable chateaux to one of the most glamorous hideaways on the whole coast - the Grand Hotel du Cap-Ferrat. It was built in 1908 and crowns the end of the peninsula. The setting could not be more magical - from the rooms, it seems like the hotel is sailing forth into the Mediterranean.

Below tumbling, subtropical gardens, I had lunch at the Club Dauphin, next to the most famous swimming pool in France, frequented over the years by le tout Riviera, including Somerset Maugham, Charlie Chaplin, Tina Turner and Elton John.

I chatted over chicken salad with Pierre Gruneberg, who has taught swimming at the hotel since 1950. His fondest memories are of Paul McCartney, and teaching the Beatle's six month-old daughter Stella (now the Paris fashion designer) to swim.

"He was a most charming man. He had enormous patience, he put a lot of love into it."

Most recently Pierre has swum with Ralph Lauren and chatted with U2 (the boys evidently taking time off from their house-cleaning rota to have a beer at the hotel). It was a good start. A magical setting, and enchanting stories of famous people.

Exhilarated by my first gulp of glamour, I headed west until the traffic jam that is St.Raphael. Everywhere I went, the traffic congestion had worsened since five years ago, when it was terrible. I fumed in the fumes for an hour before reaching the gulf of St.Tropez, where the snarl-up was just as epic but at least I could spend my time counting Porsches. Once in St.Trop (the French nickname, meaning 'St. Too-Much') I wandered along the port where old codgers lounged on Harley Davidsons and young bucks preened in front of 12-metre yachts, gathered for the weekend's Rolex Challenge race.

Rolex, yachts, old codgers on Harleys. All it needed was beautiful girls. Needless to say there were gaggles of them, all tall, all dandelion thin, all reared in the art of knowingly ignoring the male gaze. I settled down for a good half hour of ogling. It seemed only fair. St.Tropez was looking better than ever. Sylvain Ercoli, new manager of its most illustrious hotel, Le Byblos, agreed.

"I wasn't convinced coming here. I had an image of a place totally overdone, pretentious, far from my values. In fact what I found is a real culture, a real quality of life and environment. The rich nowadays want such tranquillity. Not the flashiness of the 80s."

He looked about him, breathing in the rich tranquillity.

"Let's face it, St.Tropez is still the most famous village in the world."

He's right. Recently St.Too-Much has rarely been out of the news. From Princess Diana's last holiday, via Fergie's toe-sucking, to Geri Halliwell's stay at George Michael's La Libanaise villa, there's no shortage of celebrity magic in this one-time sardine-fishing port.

One conjurer of such magic is DJ Jack E, spin-doctor at the Byblos Hotel's Caves du Roy - the most famous nightclub in France, at least according to Jack, and he counts George Michael and Bruce Willis amongst his friends, so who am I to argue? He'd hosted Naomi Campbell's birthday at the club two weeks previously.

"It was like turning on the telly," he beamed. "They were all here - Duran Duran, Kate Moss, Oasis."

Caves du Roy gets going at 1am. The clientele are depressingly beautiful. I clung to the walls, sipping my 130 franc (£13) beer as if finishing it would bring about my instant demise. Ruud Gullit was there, bopping away with a tall blonde (he can dance; I never doubted it). So was Eagle-Eye Cherry, the American rock star, sitting still, looking intense. The decor of the club was far from inspirational (more Rochdale than Ritz) but there was no denying the spirit. Women danced on tables like dervishes, including a six foot skinny teenager in gold lamé dress and gold skull cap. I tried to dance with her but she shone too brightly. Once again I needed sunglasses.

My last two days took me to perhaps the most glamorous haunt of all, the Hotel du Cap in Antibes. I drove up to the entrance in my Fiat Punto, without sunglasses. The valet looked at me as if I'd just killed his mother.

The Hotel du Cap is for those with serious cash - literally, since the hotel refuses credit cards. With suite 644, preferred by Tom Cruise, Madonna and Clint Eastwood, going for £1,700 a night, it's best to bring large denominations. As I checked in, an Italian was settling his bill, throwing down 500 franc notes like a croupier dealing cards.

F. Scott Fitzgerald visited the hotel in its 1920s heyday, subsequently transforming it into the 'Hotel des Etrangers' in Tender is the Night. Not much has changed since - the 'flushed facade' and 'deferential palms' are still there. It remains 'a summer resort of notable and fashionable

people'. A sweeping driveway plunged down to the sea, wide enough for six Fiats, or a couple of Ferraris. The 22 acres of gardens were tropically luxuriant. By the pool a Russian whispered into a mobile phone and several glamorous children shrieked glamorously in plummy English accents and Californian drawls. A woman sunbathed wearing an immense hat that would not have been out of place at a royal wedding.

Here, clearly, were modern day versions of Fitzgerald's characters, with their 'expensive simplicity.' So long as you have the right bank balance, life at the Hotel du Cap is luxuriously straightforward. The most secretive clients book into one of the 34 cabanas at the quieter southern end with their own pool and beach. I never saw them. But then to experience true glamour, like all forms of magic, is to experience this tension between the seen and unseen, between illusion and reality. The illusion of the Hotel du Cap is that there is no one here. The reality is, everyone who's anyone is here.

The King of the Cap is hotel director Jean-Claude Irondelle, a deeply tanned, bright-eyed humorist in the Frank Sinatra mould.

"We offer something no one else does," he says. "A quality of service."

The key to such service, affirms Irondelle, is "human contact." Thus there are 240 employees for 200 guests.

"I have a familiarity with my clients other managers do not. I talk to everyone. It's about friendship, taking time."

He is doing something right - during the Cannes Film Festival studios and stars fight for rooms, sometimes literally, and in high season the world's tycoons stay for up to two months at costs of between £20,000 and £40,000.

Irondelle's conversation is laced with famous names - George Bush, Michael Douglas, Sean Connery, Sharon Stone. It's clear who's his favourite. Bill Cosby, the American comedian, comes to the hotel every August. Irondelle showed me a triangular sign Cosby made as a joke for the front desk. On one side it reads;

"Credit cards are not accepted!"

It then flips over to read: "No we are not kidding!"

The final side reads: "No I don't know what you're going to do about it!"

Irondelle's principles - no credit-cards, no TVs or mini-bars in the rooms, room service by bell rather than by telephone, seem to belong to another age, something he affirms.

"You must live here as it was 100 years ago. Time doesn't have an effect on the Hotel du Cap."

It's clear Irondelle believes there's still a cachet to the Riviera. He sees it every day. As he says, he is perhaps the last guardian of glamour on the Côte.

"If I don't believe that such luxury is going to survive, who will? My philosophy is that there will always be 200 clients in the world to come to the Hotel du Cap."

Is the Riviera still glamorous? You might as well ask does the sun still shine and the sea still sparkle, because sun and sea will always combine to attract the wealthy. And wealth breeds glamour. The unattainable.

As the rest of the world becomes more like Florida, places like Cap Ferrat, St.Tropez and Cap d'Antibes will only become more glamorous. If you win the lottery this weekend, there are worse places to spend your millions. Just one thing. Remember your sunglasses.

Glamour Planning

Local Web Resources

beyond.fr/links/cote.html
Extensive links for all towns & cities in the Cote d'Azur covering culture, education, food & wine, lodging, media, nature, sports, travel and more. Also has a great calendar of events happening all over the region and individual pages on all towns and villages.

angloinfo.com
English 'What's On' site with information on arts, sports, dance, conferences and events on the Cote d'Azur with direct links to local tourist offices. For example: cannes-on-line.com, monaco-congres.com; saintpaulweb.net

crt-riviera.fr/crt-riviera/crt/menu_english.html
English version of the official Riviera Regional Committee of Tourism webpage.

rivieraworld.com
Useful directory of Riviera links.

Events and Entertainment

festival-cannes.fr
The official site of the Cannes International Film Festival.

nicecarnaval.com
Multilingual official website of the Carnival de Nice.

Glamour Sport

Golf
Some of the world's top golf architects, Pete Dye, R T Jones Sr &

Jr, and Bob Von Hagge have designed courses in the French Riviera:

Royal Mougins G.C. - a Bob Von Hagge championship course ranked in Europe's Top 50 that hosts the European Tour's Cannes Open.
Cannes Mougins G.C. - a private and exclusive Peter Allis design.
Barbaroux G.C. - Pete Dye's first course in France, also ranked in Europe's Top 50.
Ste. Maxime G.C. - a spectacular hillside course with several greens perched overlooking the Mediterranean.
St. Endreol G.C. - heralded as "the new king of southern France's golf courses".
Monte Carlo G.C. - host to the European Tour's Monte Carlo Open, offering mountain golf at its best. For golf packages featuring these clubs see golfawaytours.com.

Yacht Charter
cannesnautic.com: Yacht charter, yacht broker and limousine service.

Yacht Club
yacht-club-st-tropez.com: Site of St Tropez's yacht club.

Helicopters
heliriviera.com: Luxury consumer company, the 'premier aviation consultancy service to the luxury yachting industry' offering helicopter sight-seeing tours, heli-golf, heli-skiing, corporate jet and seaplane charter and sales.

Hotels and Villas

cote-dazur-hotels.com
For general Cote d'Azur hotel listings, with good images.

cannes-hotels.com
The official website for the association of hoteliers in Cannes.

cotedazurvillas.co.uk
Villa rental in the South of France

Hotels mentioned in Jim Keeble's Article
Grand Hotel Cap Ferrat: grand-hotel-cap-ferrat.com
Hotel du Cap and Eden Roc: edenroc-hotel.fr

Recommended Reading

Cadogan Cote d'Azur Guide
Publisher: Cadogan Books. ISBN: 1-86011-976-X

The Royal House of Monaco : Dynasty of Glamour, Tragedy and Scandal by John Glatt. St. Martin's Press. ISBN: 0312193262

Riviera Style - From the Cote D'Azur to the Amalfi Coast and the island of Capri by Dianne Verger. ISBN: 1902686012

French Riviera: The 20s and 30s by C. Bilas et al. ISBN: 2745000519

Impressions of the Riviera: Monet, Renoir, Matisse and Their Contemporaries by Kenneth Wayne (Editor). ISBN: 0916857123

THINGS TO DO 'BEFORE YOU DIE' NO. 415

The Dordogne
"Watch the sunset in the tiny stone chapel at Le Petit Jumilhac, when the burning orange sun streams through the door and lights up the altar. It may inspire you to break into hymn. 'The Lord's My Shepherd' (original version) is recommended." *Sue Carpenter*

La France Profonde

La France Profonde

Driving is one way to access what the French call *La France Profonde* - deepest France. But it will be fleeting - after all, you're in a car. The best way is to rent a house. This gives you time and leisure to explore the region, taste the food, shop in the markets and, above all, sleep in a French house, the older the better. Hotels just don't do it. You need to hear creaking pipes, noises in the orchard and smell cheese in the larder to get anywhere near La France Profonde.

Self-catering holidays in France have exploded in the last decade, especially amongst the British. It is partly the fact that so many properties have been bought up by foreigners, as France still provides some of the best value rural property in Western Europe if you take into account ease of access and quality of life. To finance the houses, they rent them out, so consequently there are now a huge range of gites, manor houses, villas and châteaux for rental all over France.

The downside is that the most popular areas can get incredibly crowded at the height of the season. Small French hilltop villages have been turned into nostalgic theme parks selling expensive jams, substandard foie gras, dubiously flavoured olive oil in inventive bottles and expensive 'local' jewellery made by 'incomers'. The narrow roads, too, will be clogged with British, Dutch and German license plates. They don't call it Dordogneshire for nothing.

Still, France is large enough and robust enough to cope. It only becomes unbearable in certain parts of the most popular areas - the Dordogne and Provence being the worst cases. Furthermore, even there the French have managed to keep their quality of life - just around the corner from the quaint restaurant with the menu in six languages will be a small local place where the French eat; every town and village will have it's weekly market, and here you'll find, alongside the smattering of stalls selling aromatherapy oil and corn dollies, dozens of others doing what they've always done, selling mounds of ripe tomatoes, honeys of all descriptions, staggering cuts of fresh meats and an abundant array of cheeses - unpasteurised. Even if there was pressure to change, the French are clever enough to know that this is what we come for - a quality of life we can only dream of back home. Renting a villa in France is still one of the best, as well as in many cases the most economic ways to experience France. Shopping in a French market for tonight's supper is an experience everyone can enjoy.

As always, it is important to do your research. Once you know where you are going, find out as much as you can about the area, where to eat, where to visit etc. Often the best places - if you are after a special meal out - will need booking before you arrive, especially in high season. Many operators and villa companies provide briefing notes, but do not always rely on them because they will not always be up to date and, in any case, you must remember that everyone else booking through that company has that same list if they are in that area. And second, choose your villa companions carefully....

Below we have two pieces to get you inspired - one on villa holidaying, another on the Luberon, a popular villa destination.

Maureen Barry

The Luberon

"Tuesday it's Carpentras craft market, Wednesday it's Apt's fantastic fruit and veg - and the cheeses just have to be seen to be believed - Thursday and Friday there's art and drama at St Rémy," my hostess rapped out her list, "then opera on Saturday at Orange and on Sunday - a special treat - the antique market at Ile-sur-Sorgue!" It was obvious that here in the Luberon, among people who know, there'd never be a dull moment whether your unfulfilled craving lay in the soul or in the stomach.

The Luberon might have remained forever a little-known area in the French Midi had it not been for the impact on the local scene of Peter Mayle and his best-selling slices of Provençal life, since when the region has become transformed by the English psyche into a Gallic sort of Larkin-land, full of amiable peasants and endearingly industrious artisans.

Marcel Pagnol's slightly more vicious interpretation of Provençal village life was perhaps nearer the mark, and cult followers of his films Jean de Florette and Manon des Sources had more francophiles hot-footing it across the Channel in search of that elusive real thing - totally un-trammeled Provençal charm.

Not surprising that they found the Luberon, a land full of unlikely curiosities, one of the most appealing corners of Provence. The range of moon-landscape hills divides at Bonnieux into the Grand Luberon to the east and the Petit

Luberon to the west. The higher and wilder Grand Luberon can still claim to be 'unknown' - from the village of Auribeau I hiked up on foot to the peak of Rourre Negre, an appetite-rousing 1,100 metres, for a breathtaking view stretching from the Rhône to the Alps.

Back in Auribeau it was napkin-tucked-under-chin time at dusk at La Besette for some thrush paté, the local speciality, then an omelette made with truffles from the Ventoux, followed by the marvellous lamb of Sisteron, the flesh subtly scented from its diet of tiny wild herbs that grow in the garrigue, with aubergines and red peppers char-grilled to intensify their sweetness, and to finish the piquant goat cheeses of valreas, picodon and banon. To drink I had a rosé from the Château Val Joanis which lies in the eponymous valley in the Luberon mountains.

But it is the Petit Luberon to the west of Apt that seems to hold the elusive essence that is for some the 'real' Provence. The name Vaucluse comes from the Latin for 'closed valley'. On one side it is flanked by the valley of the Rhône with its vineyards and on the other by the Durance, with the white-topped Mount Ventoux rising majestically over the predominant tones of deep purple, orange and green - Cezanne's colours and country. This is a fecund land of swelling grapevines and luxuriant vegetable plots, honey-coloured villages clinging to steep hillsides alongside a protective château, fields of waving lavender and scattered everywhere the wild herbs that spread the pervasive perfume that is the classic scent of the Midi.

The first inhabitants of the Luberon, the Vaudois, were a pretty wild bunch who were over-fond of pillaging and general shenanigans, so much so that a medieval Royal Crusade had most of them rather gruesomely thrown out.

Today the area attracts a different kind of settler. It has become just about the most popular corner of France for actors, intellectuals, politicians and others, not just the French who have bought second homes here, but francophiles from all over the world who have bought old properties, especially around Bonnieux, Menerbes, Gordes and other hill villages. This might have changed the Luberon's social character - in fact some of the liveliest cocktail parties in the world are held hereabouts - but it hasn't done anything to interfere with the natural beauty of the landscape. Very wisely no new building is permitted - and although old buildings can be converted a very vigilant conservation lobby makes sure that villages preserve their outward aspect. Of course this has pushed house prices up and added to the area's trendiness.

"Sur le pont, d'Avignon..." Every schoolchild knows the ancient nursery rhyme and, though the capital of the Vaucluse was the seat of the Popes in the 14th century, everybody has heard of its 'pont' and more recently its summertime drama festival. For this land is a culture vulture's dream - small wonder it attracts so many of the cognoscenti. Exquisite examples of Roman, Romanesque and Gothic architecture are scattered between Avignon and Digne, and so many towns hold art festivals in the summer months that you'd be hard-pressed to visit them all. Since the war the Luberon has been the main focus of cultural life in Provence and has boasted such talents as the writers Camus and Julio Cortazar, the photographer Henri Cartier-Bresson, the abstract artists Andre Lhote and Nicholas de Stael, the op-artist Vaserely whose museum is at Gordes and the now highly fashionable English creator of life-sized terracotta reliefs, Raymond Mason.

Make sure that you're in Châteauneuf-du-Pape on the first weekend in August and have a gloriously tipsy time at the Fête de la Veraison, when they celebrate the changing of the grape colour from green to red with an antiques fair and medieval craft market, all done with inimitable French panache. Only a few days later I sat in evening dress in the Roman amphitheatre at Orange and listened to Verdi; the combined spell of the setting, the Provençal night and the singing lifted opera into another dimension.

"Carpentras in November..." I was told. Every town has its season, its time to show off the skills of its artists and artisans. The arts and crafts fair in Carpentras has been pulling in the crowds in November for the last 460 years quite an impressive record. And if you miss that one but can manage to be there in January, February or March your nose will tell you that you've come to the truffle fair.

Don't miss the Provençal festival in Bollene in September, another excuse for much tippling and eating of local specialities, like a mouth-scorching aioli, or a pistou soup based on vegetables and a purée of garlic and basil, or one of the many game dishes from the mountains: hare, pheasant or chamois. Apt, in the Grand Luberon, is famous for its candied fruit and its Saturday morning market that sings with colour from the cornucopia of plenty groaning on its stalls. If you are here in December you must visit the Salon des Santonniers, where the carved wooden figures known as santons are made and sold. Carving wooden furniture and santons is a speciality in the Luberon, it used to be the shepherds' hobby on the long evenings when the sheep had come down from the pastures for winter and now it's a very welcome source of supplementary income.

One of the most romantic places in the whole of the

Luberon is the Fontaines de Vaucluses, where water from underground chasms rises dramatically to the surface. This is the spot where Petrarch used to come and pine for his Laura, surely the greatest unrequited love in history. In an attempt to find out the legendary depth of the source Jacques Cousteau sent a diver; he never returned and the source to this day retains its mystery. Not far from the Fontaines is Baume-de-Venise, home of the exquisite dessert wine, made from the *pourriture noble*, noble rot, of the late autumn grapes, the distillation of summer in one heady bottle.

Lovely as the Petit Luberon still is, if you want to find La France Profonde it is more likely to be found among the hills of rippling lavender of the Grand Luberon, with the winding trails of the shepherds and their stone *bories* leading you on to small villages where time has left no mark on the architecture or way of life. On the way you can peer with awe at the most beautiful limestone gorge in Europe, the Gorges de Verdon, and stop at all costs at Moustiers-la-Marie, whose renowned potters made a dinner service for Louis XIV at Versailles. But then head for the heights of the Valensole plateau, see the wonder of the Luberon spread out before you and feel the inspiration that has drawn many artists to live and work in this especially blessed corner of France. There is no better place to stop and spend time.

Nigel Tisdall

―――――

GASCONY VILLA

It began, like all good things, with a boozy Sunday lunch with friends. "Why don't we all get a villa in the south of France this year?" someone suggested. The idea spread through us like a tot of cognac slips down on a chill morning. Yes! A château on a hill, with a pool and a long garden, and almond croissants for breakfast. What about June half-term? The men frowned. They thought of the cost, the need to get euros, the crowded autoroutes. How will I get everything into the boot? And the south of France? Wasn't it just full of wine snobs in cravats, and Peter Mayle types buying up fields of lavender? The women, of course, were much more positive. They could already see the kids running on the lawn in sailor suits, and dreamed of long afternoons reading Sebastian Faulks under a walnut tree. There would be lots of crumpled white linen, straw hats and denim dungarees, bare shoulders in the Mediterranean sun... Being the host, it fell to me to progress this fantasy. "I'll look into it" I said boldly.

Three thousand tons of brochures later, I felt stressed. Where to go? When? How much to spend? "Now we know" sighed my wife, Alice, "why some families just go to Club Med year after year."

Our once-enthusiastic friends were dithering. Johnny might be away in June, Suzy was setting up a business and a bit short of cash. "Sod it, let's just book somewhere!" I said. "Someone will come." But who? And what if the house was awful? What would everyone think of us? And say it rains...

"It'll still be France" Alice rallied. "We'll just get lots of wine and get merry."

We chose Gascony because it is hardcore rural France, and virtually free of tourists. It's also a doddle to get there flying into Toulouse, and we crossed our fingers that it would be warm and sunny by early June. We then plumped for Domaine du Luc, a huge six-bedroomed manor house near Auch, purely because it had a lovely creeper-clad façade and a big front lawn.

"We've rented this fab mansion in France" I would casually let slip down the pub, "if you fancy it." At the same time Alice would be in a wine bar, enthusing about this idyllic French villa we've just found - you really should come. Later, back at home, we would stomp about in our dressing gowns yelling at each other. Why on earth did you invite Patsy? Don't you realise Max's kids are a pair of psychopaths? And what will happen if everyone we've invited says yes? They'll be hanging from the terracotta tiles. It's all going to be une grande nightmare...

Well it wasn't, though you must be prepared for chopping and changing, even last minute cancellations. In the end there were thirteen of us - four couples plus five children aged three to ten - and most of us had never met before. Inviting friends of friends might seem a risky business, but I'd recommend it because you meet new people and have plenty to talk about. Our party included two Danes, who drove at breakneck speed from Copenhagen and brought a laptop that had been specially programmed to identify the stars that would twinkle above our little bit of France that week. We also had a constantly happy Australian. In future we will always pack an Australian male when we go on holiday - they always demand to be put in charge of the barbecue, which is fine by us, and they will spend hours playing sporty games with your kids.

It was only when we arrived at Domaine du Luc that I realised what a hit-and-miss game renting villas is. This wasn't just because the instructions to find it were useless - that's par for the course on a holiday like this - but because of the location. Dutifully clad in its creepers, the house was much grander than its photo suggested, and it lay tucked away at the end of a winding country lane. Beyond its sloping lawns, dappled with lemon, plum and cherry trees, were fields flecked with poppies and a horizon crowned by the steeple of Jegun village church, which was floodlit at night.

The sense of natural isolation was overwhelming. The kids could run around and play in complete safety, the house was big enough for everyone to find a private corner, and there were no Brits over the next hedge braying about the last time they tried to park at Tesco Metro.

There are two types of villa you can rent - those that are permanently let out, where the decor is sometimes sterile and/or knackered - and the privately-owned holiday home. We had the latter, which means you get the owners' taste, style and family photos on the mantelpiece. At Domaine du Luc the only drawbacks were the beds were damp and uncomfortable, and the bathrooms had the family's bits and bobs hanging around. On the plus side, we did get to play with their toy cars, raid the garage to borrow their inflatable hippo, and the kitchen came ready-stocked with things like coffee filter papers, herbs and tins of tomatoes that we could replace later. Well, we meant to replace them, honest. "It's so much better when you gang together!" one of us exclaimed on the first day. "You can get a much grander property, the kids have friends to play with, and you don't have to spend all your time cooking or cleaning up."

But what do you do on a villa holiday? Well, you eat and drink, talk and sunbathe, perfect your underwater handstands, go for a short country walk that turns into an SAS marathon because you get completely lost... The culture vultures among us took off to see the 12th century Cistercian abbey at Flaran, and the grimy cathedral in Auch, which is famous for its carved oak choir stalls full of devilish figures. Gascony is also dotted with castles and fortified towers that loom over the fields like visiting spacecraft, and it has its fair share of those little museums the French do so well. One not to miss is the delightful Bleu de Lectoure, a former tannery in Lectoure which tells the story of pastel, a plant that was used to make a pale blue dye that was world-famous in the 17th century.

This being la France profonde, food and wine was a prime concern. In a large party, you have the fun of industrial scale catering - scrambled oeufs for 20, yes I'd like to buy that strawberry gateau as big as a mini-roundabout. We were in the Gers, the undulating heartland of Gascony, where every housewife knows 1001 things to do with a goose. Salade gersoise, made with gizzards, is a local speciality, and the region is famous for its foie gras, garlic and melons. This is also armagnac country, and the home of floc, made from armagnac and grape juice. Mix this with the sparkling wine Blanquette de Limoux, which costs less than £2 a bottle, and you have the perfect aperitif for when a child messenger arrives from the poolside with the news that "the Mummys want a little something to go with the sunset".

Each night a different couple would elect to be dinner monitor, which proved a brilliant system. One night you had to give a dinner party for 13, then for the next three nights you were a guest at a dinner party for 13. This always took place outside on the terrace, under the vines and stars, just like in the Sunday supplements. Each day the cooking got a little more elaborate - an extra course of asparagus here, some quality champagne there - and the dining table soon resembled a scene from those French films where everyone just sits around eating and talking about love till the final credits roll.

One afternoon we took off in our finery for The Big Lunch, which was held in Lectoure on the terrace of the Hotel de Bastard (cue giggles in the back of the car). It's not very far from the small town of Condom (cue more giggles), which we would often slip into for some safe shopping. And yes, everything there really is sold in packets of three. The food at de Bastard was outstanding, and continuing proof that you can still dine like a roi in France's unsung corners. The children sat at their own table, chattering through a menu enfant for under a fiver that was gracefully served on blue and white Limoges porcelain. Meanwhile the men ploughed through exquisite plates of foie gras, lamb and duck, helped along with the rich local wine, Madiran. The women saved themselves for the formidable desserts - blini de chocolat, a featherlight soufflé made with prunes and armagnac...

And the kids? What kids? In a big villa you hardly see them, though you know someone has an eye on them. Being in a group also means you can dump them on fellow guests if you want to pop off to a market or go for a walk à deux. Now and again I would come across my seven year-old son and say "have you written your postcard to granny yet?", to which the usual reply was a splash followed by two disappearing flippers. With a huge garden, a pool and Sky

TV, they were all in junior heaven. We had meant to get the TV hidden away before arriving but forgot - one child, fearing withdrawal symptoms, had watched six episodes of The Simpsons in a row before agreeing to come to the airport with us.

At the end of the week I suddenly became concerned that we hadn't paid much attention to our ten year-old daughter, Lilia. Look Dads, why are we opening another bottle of wine when we should be giving piggybacks in the pool? Aren't holidays supposed to be about family bonding and all that? Alice did some research. "Daddy's worried we haven't spoken to you all week." "Yes, I know" Lilia replied, "it's been brilliant."

That probably explains why, when I suggested a trip to the Pyrenees on our last day, there were only three contenders - one of which was a forcibly enlisted three year-old. Well, the sun was shining, and everyone had got into a lazy groove. The Pyrenees will be there another day. Within 90 minutes' drive we were in another world, climbing up the Valle d'Aure to bracing air and snow-patched mountains. We bought a picnic of bread and Pyrennean cheeses, and followed the hairpins to Col du Tourmalet on roads daubed with supportive messages left over from the Tour de France. Up at nearly 7,000 feet, we found a Bondish world of bright sunshine, empty ski resorts and pockets of grass where fawn-coloured cows tinkled their bells amid the wildflowers.

"Snow everywhere" three year-old Poppy declared like some trainee Michael Fish.

The next day it was all over, though clearing up is pretty quick when there are lots of you. A heavily laden vehicle was dispatched to the bottle bank, and as soon as our convoy of cars headed for the airport it started to rain heavily. Phew, I thought. You need a bit of luck to have a great villa holiday, but we'll be doing it again this year. Maybe a big farmhouse in Italy, with around 20 of us - let me know if you fancy it...

Villa Rental

Vintage Travel
Small specialist tour operator based in Cambridgeshire, "entirely dedicated to winkling out houses with private pools in those natural landscapes that are culturally distinct and that will reward you with new discoveries." In France they have a high quality selection of houses sleeping between 2 and 10 people.
Tel: 01954 261431; See vintagetravel.co.uk

VFB Holidays
Busy, well known and long-established operator dealing in self-catering gítes throughout rural and coastal France, to suit all tastes and chosen for their character and style. Tel: 01242 240340; See vfbholidays.co.uk

Dominiques Villas
London based company offering selection of 140 hand-picked villas and chateaux with private pools throughout the Southeast, Midwest and Southwest of France, including the Languedoc-Rousillon region featured in our articles. Tel: 020 7738 8772

frenchconnections.co.uk/chateaux/index.html
Extensive list of chateaux and manoirs available for private rental or offering bed & breakfast style accommodation, with good information and photos of all properties.

preferredplaces.co.uk/france.cfm
Preferred Places provide an easy-to-navigate database creating a link between private owners of self-catering accommodation of all sorts in France and holidaymakers in Britain, enabling direct bookings with owners.

gascony-secret.com
You can see photographs and book La Domaine du Luc, where
Nigel Tisdall stayed, from The Gascony Secret, an operator
offering self-catering accommodation in South West France.
Tel: 01284 827253

Local Resources

provenceguide.com
Good site (though slow to load) with extensive information on all
local festivities and markets in the Vaucluse region with dates,
descriptions and contact details. Search for details of the annual
truffle, apricot and lavender festivals, or find out which markets
happen in which towns and on which days.

provenceweb.fr
Good information resource for the villages and districts of
Provence with photos, descriptions, historic sites to visit,
suggested activities, festivals, markets and crafts. Also maps,
hotels, campsites and real estate.

luberon-news.com
General information on the gastronomy, accommodation, and
culture of the Luberon, with pages for individual towns & villages,
real estate listings and other useful addresses.

Related Reading

Markets of Provence : A Culinary Tour of Southern France
by Dixon Long, Ruthanne Long. Collins Publishers San
Francisco. ISBN: 0002250616

The Most Beautiful Villages of Provence by Michael Jacobs,
Hugh Palmer. Thames and Hudson. ISBN: 0500541876

Travelling through History: The Lure of the South

The Lure of the South

France has long enjoyed a rich artistic tradition, and nowhere is this truer than in painting. It is partly a result of example, France being a leading importer of new styles and traditions, both from Renaissance Italy and elsewhere; partly of opportunity, as the French court was for a long time one of the foremost patrons in Europe. But perhaps mostly it is a result of temperament - the French are a visual, image-concious people, and painting has always been part of their blood.

We can see the results today in the great collections of the Louvre and the Musée d'Orsay in Paris. But travelling in France also gives us an unrivalled opportunity to get into the mind of the painter, because one of the most fertile periods of French art history, as well as one of the most accessible to the modern mind, was the period 1860 to 1920, the age of the impressionists and post impressionists. These men and women took as their starting point the natural landscape and surroundings of rural as well as metropolitan France in reaction to the stiff classical landscapes of the imagination that had gone before. Any visitor to Arles today is able to stand at the very spot where Vincent Van Gogh painted the famous yellow and blue Café de la Nuit and virtually see the painting coalesce in front of him. And driving across the pungent, arid landscape of Provence in summer, try half closing your eyes (engine switched off, naturally) and visualising the landscape the way Paul Cézanne did. The strong colours - deep cypress green, ochre red, the dull grey of the rocks - break up into a kaleidoscope of flat shapes, and suddenly you are there with Cézanne on the very threshold of modern art, where natural shapes and colours become abstract and it's a short step to Pablo Picasso and George Braques.

There are few areas of France so intimately connected with painters in France than the south - Provence, the Côte d'Azur (where many of their works still adorn the walls of what was then their local café, the Colombe d'Or) and the coast down towards Spain. The light was what inspired them, creating all those strong colours and shapes and besides, perhaps there was a more prosaic reason: the climate.

The south is also attractive as a destination for its history. Standing at the crossroads of a number of cultures, the *Languedoc* has never had an easy relationship with the north. Castles are more abundant here than almost anywhere else in France. While Martin O'Brien follows the trail of the artists, James Henderson explores the much earlier history of the Cathars...

James Henderson

The Cathars

The story of the Cathars, 12th century heretics from southern France, has inspired more occultists, esoteric adepts, re-incarnationists, anthroposophists, treasure seekers (and one finder, apparently), writers and artists (Wagner among them) and general mystics than a poor sceptic could shake a stick at.

It has an illustrious mystic pedigree: druids, alchemists, gnostics, the Knights Templar and Rosicrucians have all had a look-in apparently, and the lost Cathar treasure - which was smuggled out of their stronghold at Montsegur when it was besieged in 1244 - has variously been thought to be the Holy Grail, the Egyptian Mysteries, the lost gospel of John, an extra-terrestrial treasure bringing unlimited wealth, even the lost bloodline of Christ (apparently he might have been alive and well and living with a family in the South of France in AD45).

Academics dismiss all this legend as febrile twaddle of course, but more than a few amateur historians have staked a lifetime's work on it. And it adds an amusing dimension to the usual pleasures - art and architecture, wine and cheese - of a holiday in France. The story hangs well on a number of medieval fortified towns and spectacular ruined hilltop castles in the foothills of the Pyrenees, itself spectacular country, ideal for exploration by car or on foot. As you head south from Toulouse the farming flatlands crumple and rise into the hills and then, rockfaces protruding as you head east, the mountains turn into the sun- and wind-burned scrubland of the Mediterranean.

In the twelfth century, Languedoc (an area larger than the simple region that it is today) was the most civilized place in Western Europe. The counts of Languedoc sponsored the troubadours, erected magnificent romanesque buildings and were even known to tolerate a certain amount of government by the people.

They also tolerated the Cathars, or the 'good Christians' as they called themselves. In notable contrast to the showy and opulent lifestyle of the Catholic Bishops, the Cathars led a frugal and simple life. They considered themselves the inheritors of the real baptism of Christ, the baptism of fire and spirit, passed down, they believed, in an unbroken line from believer to believer since the Last Supper.

But as dualists their heresy (history has been written by the victors of course) was enough to spur the Pope into action and he promptly sent a crusade. In 1209 Simon de Montfort, envoy of the Northern French king (who had an eye on the prosperous southern lands which would extend his territory to the Mediterranean) descended on the south. It was a cruel age. "How shall we tell a Catholic from a heretic?" ran the question when the crusaders reached Beziers. "Kill them all", replied the abbot, "the Lord will recognize his own." An estimated 20,000 people were slaughtered.

The crusaders razed the country, passing from one fortified town to the next. They are still attractive towns - some still have their fortifications and narrow streets of stone houses topped with terracotta Italian-style roof tiles. Carcassonne, still with superb walls and turrets, fell in a week, and then they moved on to Minerve, where the houses huddle on a small spit of land surrounded by deep river gorges. By this time the invaders had come up with another arrangement - those who recanted would be spared, after a visit to the Inquisition, but for unrepentant heretics it was the stake. At Minerve 140 decided to be burned alive.

Eventually they wound up at the walls of Toulouse, the senior county of the Languedoc. Toulouse is still an unofficial capital of the south and if you're not one to arrive on horseback with a retinue of knights then you can still expect a hospitable welcome. It is probably the best place from which to explore the area. Toulouse is a cosmopolitan town again - more than just the Moors and Jews of the 12th century are there now of course; Vietnamese and North African restaurants line the red brick streets.

It wouldn't quite be true to say that the Inquisition was invented to combat the Cathars, but it was the first time that they really got into gear. As the Frankish northerners consolidated their political power, picking off the towns, so the Dominican Inquisitors, based in Toulouse, sought out the heretics with greater fervour. The beleaguered Cathars retreated south into the Pyrenees, holing up in the fortress castles of sympathetic lords.

I followed them, mystic divining sticks twittering in anticipation. As the terrain rises into the mountains around Foix, so the fertile earth thins and fir and spindly birch trees cling to the hillsides beneath the cold grey faces of the massifs. The castles each sit squat on top of a massive promontory of rock, visible for miles around. They are all ruined now, but they are mostly accessible and they are ideal for those who enjoy rootling around abandoned castles - donjons and curtain walls with man-size battlements, barbicans, jousting grounds and catapult platforms.

The Cathar stronghold and the centre of their faith was

Montsegur, a looming grey colossus which stands on a huge outcrop at 1200 metres, so vast that as you climb the last few hundred feet on switchback paths among boxwood bushes, its walls seem to lean into the moving clouds. Montsegur is a deserted shell now (except for the odd neo-Cathar soaking up the vibes), so sad and empty, and it takes an effort to imagine the desperation of the siege in 1244, when it saw the self-immolation of a religion. The Cathars held out here for nearly a year, but after their treasure was secure (carried down the cliffs of the north side of the mountain) they surrendered. 225 of them went willingly to their deaths on a blazing stockade.

The treasure, whatever it was, was supposedly taken south via other strongholds to the caves of the high Pyrenees. I passed Roquefixade, perched atop its massive rock, over-looking pastures that echoed with the bells of mountain cat-tle. Further south, Lordat stands ruined on its vast rock, its barbican and concentric defensive walls now breached and its dilapidated stonework wrapped in dead roots like brittle brown lace.

The castle at Montaillou, further east, is in even sorrier repair - just a few rubble stone walls remain - but the village has immortality in another way, recorded by Emmanuel Le Roy Ladurie in 1978. Montaillou tells of life in a medieval village at the time when these castles were built. It was written from notes made by the Inquisition in the early 1300s, when they were hounding the last of the Cathars (the book mentions the last known French Cathar initiate, Guillaume Belibaste, who was burned to death in 1321). The rest fled to Lombardy and to the Balkans where Catharism survived until the invasion of the Ottoman Turks in the 15th century.

Others believe that the treasure made its way east, through the sheer-sided gorges where the rockface rises sheer for a thousand feet, to the parched Mediterranean mountains, where the Corbiere vineyards and clusters of orange roofs stamp the only human patterns into the boxwood and myrtle scrubland. A string of brooding stone monsters covers the approaches from Spain but they were picked off steadily by the crusaders: Puylaurens, a saw-toothed crown on a peak, a castle and stronghold large enough for a short golf hole and Peryepertuse, which sprawls along a ridge, its redoubts on the different peaks linked by battlements. My favourite is Queribus, a clifftop fortress guaranteed to taunt any invader. It stands massive, square and grey, with the winds whistling around it, defying anyone to attack it.

But the favoured resting place of the Cathar treasure is the hilltop village of Rennes le Chateau to the north. In the last century a priest supposedly discovered it, or part of it at least. Mysteriously he became immensely wealthy. He left his mark in buildings around the village and in a huge following of amateur sleuths. Unfortunately for the inhabitants they have obviously been digging it up - there is actually a sign saying: 'Archaeological Excavations Forbidden'.

Even Rennes le Chateau failed to reveal the supernatural secrets of ancient Languedoc to the poor sceptic - though the car radio took a mystic turn when it whispered elliptical allusions as it went in and out of tune in the mountains - but perhaps you will have more luck. Maybe a hooded mystic will emerge from a carved doorway in a mountain village and give you an ecstatic look of recognition, make a cabalistic greeting and say: "Ah, you have arrived at last.... We have been waiting for you.... for many centuries...."

Martin O'Brien

Art and Artists

Wherever you are in Provence it doesn't take long to realise that you recognise this country, that its distant perspectives, its bright splashes of colour and creeping blue shadows, its bold shapes and patterned landscapes are all distinctly familiar. Walk, as I did, along pine-needle paths in the hills above the sail-speckled Golfe de St Tropez, or set out across the sunflower plains around Arles, or through the orchards and vineyards of Aix-en-Provence, and that sense of déjá vu is as strong as a slug of eau de vie. Which is hardly surprising, for this sun-drenched land of angular red roofs, dagger-like cypresses, picture-postcard ports, vine-braided valleys and brooding massifs has inspired many of the world's greatest artists.

On every road leading towards Aix-en-Provence the motorist is advised that the countryside he is driving through is Les Paysages de Cezanne. Not that he should need any telling. Dominated by the pewter-coloured peak of Montagne Sainte Victoire which so inspired Cezanne, the landscape is never less than strikingly familiar. Drive east from Aix towards Le Tholonet and Puyloubier, or south into the Arc Valley, and the references become increasingly hard to miss. As well as savouring these eerily familiar landscapes - their stark shapes and shifting colours - you can also visit the atelier Cezanne built for himself in 1897 in what are now the city's northern suburbs or, alternatively, wander through the grand salons of the Musee Granet in Aix itself where he took his first drawing classes. Housed in a former priory of the Knights of Malta, the Granet collection ranges from local archaeological remains, appropriately displayed in the basement, to classics by Ingres, Gericault, David, Largilliere and, of course, by the Master of Aix himself.

If Aix and its countryside belongs to Cezanne, then Arles, that ancient town on the banks of the Rhone, proved equally inspiring for Van Gogh. In Arles itself there is little to see of the places Van Gogh painted (the town's famous bridge and the house where he lived were destroyed in the war) but outside town the fields of sunflowers, the swaying speartip cypresses, the wheeling crows and distant ridges of the Alpilles vividly recall his intense and startling vision.

Although Van Gogh completed more than three hundred paintings during his brief stay, not a single work remains in Arles. But what the town lacks in Van Gogh, it makes up for with one of Provence's finest ethnographic museums. Started by the Provencal writer Frederic Mistral in 1896 and majestically housed in the 16th century Palais Laval-Castellane, the Museon Arlaten is like a key to the soul of Provence. In curtained salons, their ancient wood floors creaking and their high ceilings lost in shadows, you will find one of the most complete accounts of everyday Provencal life - just as Mistral knew it. Delightfully patrolled by attendants in traditional Arlesian costume, the Museon's 30 rooms cover every aspect of Provencal life, so crowded with exhibits that you could spend a week here. Mistral may not have saved the language of Provence, but he has preserved its traditional way of life with this captivating collection, "a poem", he once remarked, "for those who don't read".

From Arles it is an easy drive north to the walled fastness of Avignon, the jewel in Provence's medieval crown. Here, behind formidable fortifications, stands the fortress-like Palais des Papes, home to seven successive French Popes whose wealth transformed this Roman river port into one of the most splendid courts in medieval Europe.

It is undoubtedly the magnificence of their former residence with its soaring towers and battlements, and the anticipation of exploring its vaulted and frescoed interior, that draws the eye away from a small three-storey building in the north corner of the Places des Papes. Called, appropriately, Le Petit Palais, and built in the fourteenth century as a residence for bishops attached to the Papal court, it now houses an appropriately ecclesiastical collection of Italian medieval and Renaissance art.

Here, in the barrel-vaulted halls and beamed salons of what is now the Musee du Petit Palais, are gilded annunciations and adorations by the score, gruesome crucifixions, massacres and martyrdoms, serene Madonnas and dimpled baby Christs, haloed saints and plump-faced angels with cheeks as pink as a Provencal rose. First assembled in the nineteenth century by Italian collector Gian Pietro Campana, the paintings and sculptures on show date from the thirteenth to the sixteenth centuries and include not only unrivalled masterpieces by Botticelli, Carpaccio and Giovanni di Paolo, but also rarely seen work by Provencal artists like Enguerrand Quarton and Josse Lieferinxe. Le Petit Palais may be smaller than its lofty neighbour, but it's where the real treasures of Avignon are to be found.

When the lure of the Provencal coast becomes too much to bear, the only good advice is surrender and head south. Bouillabaisse, beaches and Bardot have all contributed to make this coastline the most celebrated in the world. And the famed Riviera of Nice and Cannes, you'll quickly discover, is only half the story. From St Tropez to the Rhone Delta this southern shoreline is a treat to savour, its delightful fishing ports, pinewood paths, rocky coves and sandy beaches as irresistable now as they were when Derain, Dufy, Picasso and Braque set up their easels at L'Estaque, Cassis and St Tropez.

No matter how many super-yachts tie up in its old port, or how many visitors swarm through its narrow streets and along its cafe-crowded quays, St Tropez is still a name to conjure with. And what magic. Stand on the ramparts of the 16th century Citadel and look across the gulf towards Sainte Maxime and the villa-freckled slopes of the Massif des Maures, and even the most jaded traveller must admit a freshening of the spirit.

Certainly it worked its spell on the painter Paul Signac When bad weather forced his yacht into St Tropez's harbour in 1892, so enchanted was he with its pastel-fronted houses and the luminous quality of the light playing along its shoreline that he promptly bought himself a villa here and invited his friends to join him. And join him they did - artists like Vlaminck, Matisse, Bonnard, Marquet, Camoin and others, their work now exhibited in St Tropez's quayside Musee de l'Annonciade. Originally a 16th century chapel where fishermen once prayed for full nets and fine weather, its walls are now covered with some of the greatest names in modern art, one of their favourite subjects the preposterously pretty port which lies beyond the chapel's open windows.

Many of these same artists, and a host of others, are displayed in the stately salons of Marseille's Musee Cantini, a few blocks from the restauraunt-lined Vieux Port and just round the corner from the art-deco Opera. Housed in a 17th century mansion, the Cantini collection traces the various movements that contributed to the evolution of modern 20th century art, from Fauvism and Cubism to Surrealism and Neo-Realism. Here are Signacs and Schnabels, Picassos and Picabias, Miros and Magnellis, more than 250 first division artists whose ranks are regularly swelled, thanks to the Cantini's energetic and imaginative approach to acquisition. Amongst the most recent arrivals are Picasso's Tete de Femme Souriante, Giacometti's Portrait de Diego and works by Matisse, Signac and Chagall. At the Musee Cantini you can bet your last sou there'll be something new and exciting to see every time you visit.

West of Marseille, across the muscular waters of the Rhone, the salty shallows of the Camargue and the vast flatlands of the Crau, lies Provence's lesser known but no less agreeable neighbour, Languedoc-Roussillon. Stretching from the weather-whipped highlands of the Cevennes to the wooded slopes of the Pyrenees, this region is one of France's undiscovered delights. Its hilltops are studded with castles, its valleys ranked with vineyards, and its ancient towns a patchwork of pantiled roofs, church spires and the leafy crowns of plane trees, marking out sun-shaded boulevards and squares.

As skylines go, Nimes has always fitted this traditional southern pattern. But now there's a newcomer in town. Where the colonnaded opera house once stood, a massive square of blue-green ice the size of a city block now shimmers in the heat. Not ice, of course, but glass, a giant cube of glass called the Carre d'Art.

I had come to Nimes to see its collection of contemporary French art, more than 300 works dating from 1960 and ranging from Neo-Realists like Klein, Arman and Hains to Supports-Surfaces artists like Viallat and Hantai. But nothing had prepared me for the collection's new home, this ice-cube square of glass and steel designed by British architect Sir Norman Foster and opened in 1993. With its cathedral-sized interior and glass central stairway, its high-ceilinged, aisle-like galleries and crypt-like libraries, Nimes' new museum is as much an attraction as the collection it houses, as unexpected and avant-garde as any work on show.

From Nimes I travelled north into the rugged highlands of the Cevennes. Dominated by the summits of Mont Lozere and Mont Aigoual at the southern-most edge of the Massif Central, this is one of Languedoc-Roussillon's most dramatic and isolated landscapes, a wild and magical place whose inhabitants shelter in the clefts and valleys of a lofty tableland, and where mysterious stone menhirs point back to a distant and shadowy prehistory. Hot and dry in summer, bitterly cold and exposed in winter, the Cevennes may be a harsh and unforgiving land but it possesses a raw, savage and inspiring beauty.

One of the best ways to understand this unique and remarkable region, designated a National Park in 1970 and covering some 600 square miles, is by visiting the Ecomusee du Mont Lozere in Le Pont-de-Montvert. As its name suggests, this is no ordinary museum. As well as describing the region's natural character and showing how man adapted to this most demanding of environments, the Ecomusee goes one step further. Beyond its walls, radiating in all directions from Le Pont-de-Montvert, is a network of well-marked roads, hiking trails and bridle-paths linking a number of traditionally built homesteads, lodges and working farms administered by the Park authorities. Taken together, the museum's permanent exhibition and the living landscape that surrounds it, the Ecomusee du Mont Lozere serves as a powerful introduction to this remote and extraordinary region.

From the heights of the Cevennes I dropped back down onto the central plains of Languedoc-Roussillon, heading for Montpellier, a stylish and vibrant university town where Rabelais and Nostradamus studied medicine. Here, on the grand, tree-shaded Esplanade de Charles de Gaulle, in a former jesuit college tucked behind the elegant facade of an eighteenth-century town house, you will find the justly celebrated Musee Fabre, probably the finest art collection outside Paris.

First assembled by the painter Francois Xavier Fabre while exiled in Florence during the French Revolution, the collection was presented to Montpellier on his return home in 1825. Substantially increased by Fabre during his remaining years, the collection includes Veronese, Zurbaran, Poussin, Ribera, Greuze and Fabre himself, as well as drawings, engravings and sculptures.

If Fabre had been alone in his generosity, Montpellier could have counted itself fortunate. But following Fabre's death the museum was further endowed by a succession of generous local patrons whose donations included works by Rubens, Teniers, Reynolds, Breughel and Bernini. The greatest of these patrons was Alfred Bruyas who, unable to paint, befriended those who could. Spending much of his family inheritance on works by Millet, Delacroix, Tassaert, Corot and, most particularly, Courbet, Bruyus built up an equally formidable collection which he too subsequently bequeathed to the Museum. Amongst the classics he collected are no less than 24 portraits of the man himself by some of the greatest artists of his day, including Bonjour, Monsieur Courbet, which shows the artist meeting his enthusiastic patron on a dusty Languedoc road.

Despite this patronage and his astute acquisitiveness, Bruyas was by no means infallible. Interestingly, he failed to take notice of Cezanne in nearby Aix, and all but ignored locally-born Frederic Bazille, a friend of Sisley, Renoir and Monet and a forerunner of the Impressionist movement. That the Musee Fabre has anything at all by Bazille is due entirely to yet another benefactor, the artist's family, whose generosity has endowed the Fabre with one of the most important collections of this artist's work.

If Montpellier owes its artistic pre-eminence to the generosity of its many patrons, then the town of Ceret, close to the Spanish border, owes its standing as "The Mecca of Cubism" to the artists who lived and worked here from the turn of the century. The first to arrive, in 1909, was the Catalan sculptor, Manolo Hugue, whose enthusiasm for this enchanting settlement in the foothills of Mont Canigou quickly attracted friends like Picasso, Braques, Juan Gris, Max Jacob and Auguste Herbin. Over the years others followed - Masson, Maillol, Chagall, Saint Saens, Dufy, Dali - lured as much by the companionship and example of their peers as by the agreeable southern climate and the range of subjects Ceret and its mountainous countryside provided. It is easy, as you walk around this pretty, tree-shaded town with its medieval battlements and bread-scented alleyways, to imagine these artists sprawled around tables at the Grand Cafe discussing their work, or writing to colleagues in praise of their new-found home.

By 1950 most of the great names in modern art had visited Ceret and when one of them, the artist Pierre Brune, suggested a museum to celebrate that fact and exhibit their work, the response was immediate. Picasso, Matisse and many others donated work and an old gendarmerie was requisitioned as a gallery. Recently extended and redesigned by Catalan architect Jaume Freixa, Ceret's new Musee d'Art Moderne re-opened in 1993, a cool, white space where some of the world's most instantly recognisable styles are gloriously exhibited, a stunning collection of modern and contemporary work that celebrates not only the artists on show but the part played by this unassuming Catalan town in the history of art.

Cultural Planning

Travel Specialists

Martin Randall Travel

Specialist cultural tour operator committed to providing escorted tours for small groups, led by expert lecturers. They offer tours based around Art, History, Architecture, Music and Archaeology, 16 of which are held in various regions of France. Tel: 020 8742 3355; See martinrandall.com

Andante Travels

Tour operator owned and managed by archaeologists, offering tours designed for those who would rather "take the wonderful view and suffer insufficient drawer space". Tel: 01722 713800; See andantetravels.co.uk

Travel off the Beaten Path

American-run travel company based in Brest in France specialising in small group cultural and speciality travel. They offer a number of tours, including 'The Best of Provence' and 'Cathar Castles of South West France'. Tel: +33 298 42 29 98; See traveloffthebeatenpath.com

Alternative Travel Group

Well respected small tour operator founded in 1979 on the principles of conservation and sustainable tourism. Runs popular 8-day 'Painters & Gardens of Provence' escorted walking tour. Tel: 01865 315678; See alternative-travel.co.uk

Local Resources

culture.fr

Official website of the Department of Culture in France.

cathares.org
French-only website dedicated to Catharism with information on Carcassone and the surrounding area, medieval maps and useful links to further sites.

circulades.com
The history of the circular medieval villages of Languedoc-Roussillon.

artchive.com
Excellent site with temporary galleries of art, links to reviews and shows, books and more than 2000 scans from over 200 fine artists.

wwar.com/categories/Museums/Countries/France
World Wide Art Resources - large gateway for links to museums and galleries in France.

musexpo.com
Find details on museums and current exhibitions showing all over France, from newspaper Le Monde's online web resource.

Recommended Reading

A Concise History of France - An up-to-date, comprehensive study of French History by Roger Price. Cambridge University Press. ISBN: 052136809X

Blue Guide: France 165 itineraries for the traveller interested in exploring historical & architectural France. By Ian Roberston. A & C Black. ISBN: 0713643315

The Road from the Past, Travelling through History in France Historical travelogue through the castles, cathedrals and monasteries of France. By Ina Caro.

Luminous Debris : Reflecting on Vestige in Provence and Languedoc. An archaeological journey through the artefact-rich regions of Provence & Languedoc. By Gustaf Sobin. University of California Press. ISBN: 0520222458

Chasing the Heretics: A Modern Journey through the Medieval Languedoc by Rion Klawinski. Ruminator Books. ISBN: 1886913382

The Cathars and the Albigensian Crusade by Michael Costen. St. Martin's Press, Inc. ISBN: 0719043328

Cezanne in Provence by Evmarie Schmitt. ISBN: 3791314513

In the Footsteps of Van Gogh by Gilles Plazy, Vincent Van Gogh, Jean-Marie Del Moral. Viking Books. ISBN: 067088250X

Artists and Their Museums on the Riviera - practical guide to 28 sites by Barbara Freed, Alan Halpern. Harry N. Abrams, Inc. ISBN: 0810927616

France But Not French: Frontier France

France But Not French

Of all the countries of Europe, France has one of the longest stretches of border. For over a thousand years its history has been about the struggle to recreate the frontiers of Charlemagne's western kingdom, itself based on the old gallic provinces of the Roman empire. The expansion has occurred piecemeal, over many centuries, radiating out from the medieval heartland of the Ile de France, as the Kings of France sought to reestablish control by means of marriage and conquest. Without the clear geographic borders of, for example, the United Kingdom, the challenge has been to integrate, both politically and culturally, these new territories into a single autonomous French state. Politically they have been remarkably successful - from Louis XIV through Napoleon to the Fifth Republic, a strong executive has centralised power in Paris, way to the north.

Culturally, however, there are still fringes of France which feel very different from the centre. Places where there is an ambiguity about the cultural mix, a result of the turbulence of the struggle to establish the nation state, which sit midway between competing claims of neighbouring states. The Alsace and Lorraine provinces, for example, along the banks of the Rhine, have changed hands a number of times in the last 150 years - many there still speak German. However, these territories are at the heart of Europe, as well as close to the centre of France and relatively easy to control. It is at the extremities that independent cultures flourish the most strongly, in some cases violently. The Pays Basque, though a smaller area than the Spanish province across the frontier, is the home of an ancient nation which pre-dates the Romans; while Corsica is a heady mix of French, Italian and Greek, a fiercely independent island society and birthplace of Napoleon which has always been hard to govern. Far from Paris, and less integral to the identity of the French nation than Burgundy or Alsace, they have managed to retain something of these differences.

For the visitor, both the Pays Basque and Corsica exert a fascination that comes from these clash of cultures. They are also - perhaps in part because of this - amongst the most unspoilt parts of the country. In an age where we are all looking for something different and unique from our holiday experiences, these two areas are two very bright colours in the mosaic that is Europe.

Daniel Scott

CORSICA

"The train is never late", jokes the beady-eyed, black-bearded station master as we wait in the middle of the Corsican mountains for it to arrive, "but the timetable is often a little wrong".

With that the little box-set electric train rattles around the corner toward Vizzavona station, looking like something out of a 1950s theme park. I clamber aboard and as the train hiccoughs away find a space among smelly fellow hikers sitting on rucksacks and French and German tourists readying their videos for the remainder of one of the world's most picturesque train journeys.

All around us are thick green forests which intermittently form a natural tunnel over the train line. Above us, soaring 2000 metres into the blue summer sky, are snow-topped granite peaks. Later, as we emerge from the cocoon of the forest, we look straight out of the train window into a series of deep rocky ravines, running silver with rivers full of melted snow.

We are in the middle of the Mediterranean's most ruggedly beautiful island, chugging our way through and around its central spine of mean, meaty mountains towards the north coast. The journey is slow - the train tootles along at less than 50 kilometres per hour and sometimes stops for herds of cows or goats crossing the line - but we don't mind. It would be indecent to hurry through scenery like this.

As the train stutters across a viaduct, high above the

valley floor, I watch the driver at the front of the carriage anxiously. He has one hand on the controls, one eye on the track ahead and is sharing a laugh over his shoulder with an over-enthusiastic train buff. Opposite me, a group of leather-skinned country folk chomp on crusty bread and runny cheese and a young woman, round-rimmed spectacles on the edge of her nose, loses herself in a book of Baudelaire's poetry.

In any case I know I am safer here than on the pot-holed Corsican roads, which curl and snarl around the island's mountains. Actually it's not so much the roads themselves that are dangerous as the way that the Corsicans drive on them, melding French impatience with Italian speed and adding an indigenous sang-froid. One day's heart failure, as vehicle after vehicle headed straight toward my hire car on the wrong side of the road - only pulling over at the last moment - was all it took to convince me to let the train take the strain.

In the carriage, my attention turns once more to the rugged foothills outside the window. We are approaching Corte, the hilltop town which was once the island's capital and remains one of the centres of Corsican nationalism.

Corsican nationalism? While the French like to call the island one of their own, the Corsicans are none too happy with the idea - despite the fact that the acme of French imperialism, Napoleon Bonaparte, was born on the island, in Ajaccio. No, they see themselves as very different from their Gallic "masters", speak their own heavily inflected dialect and seem closer to the Italians just across the gulf of Genoa than they do to the French.

I also detect in them something of the Moorish and the Spanish, which is not too ridiculous an observation. After all, in its time, Corsica has been invaded by the Phoenicians, Greeks, Etruscans, Phoceans, Carthaginians and Romans, and has been ruled over by the Papacy, the Tuscans, the Aragonese, the Genoese, the Germans and even the English.

But as we meander northwards to the coastal resort of Calvi, it is the Italian influence which is the most striking. Nearly all the names of the more or less deserted mountain stations we pass through - from Francardo through Ponte Leccia, where we change onto an even smaller train, to Novella and Palasca - are quintessentially Italian.

Then, almost without warning, the train rounds a hill-side and we are heading straight for the sparkling Mediterranean sea, toward the town of Ile Rousse. Finally we follow a craggy coastline to Calvi, the train line wedged between the foot of the mountains on one side and the gently lapping ocean, metres below, on the other.

Calvi is both where my visit to Corsica began and where it will shortly end. Ten days earlier, I had arrived in the town to rendezvous with some adventurous British friends. Our plan was to tackle the Grande Route 20, the walking trail which begins at the nearby hilltown of Calenzana and traverses the mountains which dominate the island.

The GR20 is billed as "Europe's most difficult walking trail" and I soon find out why. As soon as we start walking uphill out of Calenzana, I wish I had done some training - walking to the mailbox, jumping on the spot, anything - because, what with carrying everything on our backs, including a job lot of dehydrated foods with names like "Curri Inna Hurry" and "Barbie's Dhal", I am soon breathless.

Things do not improve as I grunt and sweat my way up around 1600 metres of ascents that morning. The sublime views are definitely worth the climb but, sadly, the further up we go the more my vision is blurring. When, eight hours later, we reach our camping spot - overlooking a steep-sided valley turned golden by the sunset - my body is in shock. That night, as I lie in my sleeping bag, I attempt the last of around three thousand stretches and propel my entire lower half into a jarring stiffening cramp from which I can barely escape.

The following day I drag my limbs through another ten hours of ascents, 800-metre descents and tricky traverses as we trek nearer and nearer the snow line. Behind us, the Mediterranean continues to glisten in Calvi's horseshoe bay. Beneath us the plunge towards untouched valleys becomes more and more sheer. Ahead of us the greys, cool greens and off-whites of the Corsican mountains spread out towards the horizon, reminding me that it will take another thirteen days to get to the end of this trail.

Then, nearing the end of the second day, I fall. Nothing too dramatic, just a potentially life-threatening trip over my own walking pole, which snaps like a wishbone. Landing in the safety of some scrub at the side of the trail, my mind is made up. My dream of ever climbing Everest, or indeed of completing the GR20, is over. I am too incompetent, too inexperienced and too unfit to be let anywhere near anything you can fall off.

It is disappointing of course but the following day I bid my adventurous friends adieu and set out to find some safer parts of Corsica. Actually, leaving the GR20, while sad, is also liberating. My only way out is to walk down to the nearest road and hitch-hike and though this is my very first attempt at it, I manage to pick up three lifts in less than an hour. By lunchtime, I am in the square in Corte, supping a cold beer and digging into a mushroom pizza.

Later, after visiting the fascinating Museum of Corsica, with its insights into the anthropological, cultural roots and 8000 year-old history of this proud island, I sit in a restaurant above the town and eat dinner. Nearby, small twittering birds are flying in mists from rooftop to rooftop. Through the mists I gaze at the powerful mountains, turned blood red by the sunset. I am glad to be down here in the safety of Corte but pleased too that I have experienced something of the might and majesty of the Corsican hills.

For the next week, I head for the island's northern coast, stopping first in the port of Bastia, the gateway to Corsica from the French mainland. Here an ancient citadel coils around an old port and bijou restaurants crowd around a modern marina. Each evening, in the waning summer sunshine, the waters of the marina light up with the reflections of the white hulls of very shiny, very expensive motor yachts.

At the expansive Grand Place de St Nicholas, adjacent to the new port, meanwhile, young couples stroll hand in hand in Italianate fashion. Elsewhere, little old ladies, dressed in black, cross themselves as they enter the cool interiors of the town's impressive baroque churches, and the cobbled market place is cleared of detritus, ready for the next day. On each of the four nights I am in Bastia, I head to the restaurants by the marina to eat sumptuous seafood, accompanied by delicious Corsican wine.

I travel next to the seaside village of St Florent, hurtling over the hills which lie between it and Bastia by small public bus. Once I recover, I meet a young Corsican who has lived and worked in Western Australia for a year and, bizarrely, speaks perfect "strine", peppering his speech with expressions like "no wackas, mate".

At his suggestion we go diving in the blue grottoes offshore. In remarkably clear Mediterranean waters, we discover several seventeenth century cannons and an undersea world which mirrors the Corsica above the water, in being craggy and rocky and surrounded by oceans of blue. Later we pay a visit to the vineyards in the foothills behind the town where Corsicans are now producing wines which are giving those on the mainland a real run for their money.

After a couple more days roaming the scraggy beaches around St Florent, it is time to meet up with my walking friends again, at the half-way point of the GR20 in the popular mountain retreat of Vizzavona.

It feels good to be among the hills once more, especially when we hike the short distance from the village up to the succession of tumbling falls known as the Cascades des Anglais. Here, amid huge boulders and fragrant woods, torrents of newly melted snow roar and rumble as they rush down from the peaks. Yet in between these gushes sit tranquil pools which brim with icy, sweet-tasting mountain water.

As I leave my friends to complete the Grande Route 20, I continue my own Corsican adventure by stepping aboard that smoke-filled little train, a journey taking me out of the indomitable mountains toward the Mediterranean sea. After a few unscheduled delays due to goats on the line, the train finally draws into Calvi at 8.30pm on a still-warm summer night. But it's not that we're late, it's just that the damn timetable's out by an hour or so again.

Fraser Harrison

At first sight French rural addresses are puzzling to the British eye. They appear to be at least a line short and the post code seems to have strayed into the wrong line. Our temporary address, for example, consists of the name of the house and then, on the next line a five-figure number and another name. Is the number the post code or an American-style street number? It is, in fact, the post code and it pinpoints the house with great precision because the second name, Lantabat, refers not to a village, but to a valley.

Lantabat is in Basse Navarre, one of the three provinces that make up the Pays Basque, which is the French part of the world populated by Basques. These three provinces lie in a row along the western Pyrenees, which also marks the border between France and Spain. In all there are seven Basque provinces, the other four lying in Spain. An old form of Basque nationalist graffiti was '4 + 3 = 1'. The province on the Atlantic coast is Labourd and it boasts two of France's most agreeable cities: Bayonne, a venerable port, and Biarritz, once famed as the resort of princes, and now famous again as the only resort in Europe where the breakers are formidable enough to attract Californian and Australian surfers. Soule, an area of caves (grottes) and gorges, is the Basque province that lies furthest inland and seems the most remote for reasons that are not entirely geographic. Basse Navarre lies between these two.

We are staying in a house that overlooks Lantabat valley

and is blessed with the delightful name Choko Ona, Basque for 'beautiful corner'. The house is surrounded by a meadow, which is being grazed by cows the colour of caramel. They are Aquitaines Blanches, big, docile creatures that can be found recumbent on the sides of narrow roads winding up the mountain-sides, as contented as they are hazardous. They rip up the juicy green grass with their purple tongues and we can hear the continual clonk of the bell attached by thick leather strap to the neck of a cow accompanied by her calf. Unless the farmer removes it, this charming bell will keep us awake tonight.

The valley drops sharply below the house to the road, which follows the sinuous course of a stream, aptly named La Joyeuse. On the other side, the valley rises to a high, rocky rim over which the clouds pour in the morning like a kind of lost surf. This is a countryside of small, immaculately tended fields and meadows, and despite the hot June sun, which is making the plastic gutters creak in pain, it is also lush and emerald, a sign of its generous, mountainous rainfall. The grass feeds a dozen flocks of sheep scattered around the valley. They form white patterns against the green that appear to have been designed by a sculptor (Richard Long, perhaps): circles, crescents, snakes and mazes. In very hot weather they crowd together, head towards the centre, squeezing into a tight swarm. They must know what they're doing, though to a non-sheep their behaviour seems quite illogical and likely to do nothing but raise the temperature. Towards the end of the afternoon, punctual as commuters, they will line up in single file and trickle along the edge of the field, taking themselves home to be milked. The patter of their hooves on the road approaching the farm sounds like rain. In due course their milk will be turned into a slightly salty hard cheese imaginatively named Brebis (French for 'ewe'), which is at its most delicious when eaten with cherry jam, another speciality of the region.

The farms are small, no more than a dozen hectares, and are easily picked out, since each is dominated by its white farmhouse. Basque architecture conforms to what you might call the Prince of Wales rule, which is - if you have a good thing don't change it. At first sight the Basque house looks as if it got lost on its way to Switzerland, because it has a low pitch to its roof and large, overhanging eaves to carry snow clear of the structure. But its most striking feature is that every one looks like its neighbour: walls painted white, corners are picked out in dressed stone and, in obedience to the local law, shutters, windows, doors and so forth painted either green or oxblood. These houses tend to be enormous, almost hamlets in themselves, and are intended to house animals and machinery, as well as extended families, under one roof. Just over the border we have seen a couple of villages, Erratzu and Arizkun (typical Basque names) that still have houses in their centres with projecting upper storeys, a very old feature, and animals stalled at street level, their heads hanging over the pavement.

The Basques themselves are a short, dark, long-nosed people of ferociously independent spirit, whose men are distinguished by an almost cuboid physique and great strength that is put to the test each summer in Force Basque, trials of strength that involve lifting boulders and hacking logs. They are famous for their cuisine and the beauty of their singing in choirs of both men and women. As this valley eloquently demonstrates, they are diligent and fastidious farmers. They are of course also famous for their berets and pelote, a game played with a hard ball against a wall that is found in every village, however small. It comes in two versions, both homicidal: one involves the use of a basket scoop that allows the ball to be hurled at lethal speeds, the other is played with bare hands. Despite their often forbidding appearance, and their warlike ways of amusing themselves, Basques are hospitable and patient with foreigners.

The sun is now at its zenith in a sky that is pure blue. Its heat has brought out a little lizard covered in Op-art stripes, which skitters across the hot stones of the terrace and pauses to peck fly spots off the leg of our plastic table. A kite, identifiable by its forked tail, keeps an eye on the farmyard where a couple of yellow dogs pant in the shade. At night they will add their barking to the cow bell's percussion, and the band will be completed by a strange species of frog that makes a noise akin to an electronic glockenspiel. Later in the afternoon, as the sun cools, we may be lucky enough to see a humming-bird moth, a creature that hovers just as it name suggests. Since it is lunchtime, or at least late enough in the morning to count as lunchtime, we open a bottle of Jurancon, a white wine of the region that is served in all the bars and hotels and is a little sweet, but delicious when cold. Lunch itself will be sausage from Spain, Bayonne ham (a coarse smoked ham), a baguette bought that morning, salad and the inevitable Brebis and cherry jam.

As our thoughts turn to these pleasures, we see another version of bon appetit expressing itself. High above the valley rim a single black shape appears, gliding motionlessly in circles. Soon there are 10 black shapes in a loose cluster, and then 30, all gliding across the sky with the same effortless grace. They are griffon vultures, huge birds, with a wingspan of two and a half metres or more, which feed off the dead sheep the farmers leave out for them to dispose of on the hill tops. For all their unsavoury dining habits, they are a magnificent sight, and this part of the Pays Basque is one of the few in France where they can be observed.

We admire them for a moment and then give our whole attention to our own lunch.

One of the best ways to see the Pyrenees is to walk. The French take their walking almost as seriously as their cycling, which means that the Pyrenees, probably the finest walking area in Europe, are well endowed with paths, trails and various well-marked and mapped Grande Randonnees. Indeed, this has been an area famous for its walkers since the Middle Ages: not far from Lantabat is the town of St Jean-Pied de Port which has always been a resting place for French pilgrims on their way to Santiago de Compostela.

Frontier Planning

Travel Specialists

Simply Corsica

A selection of properties for those who want to escape the crowds and get off the beaten track - with a choice of seaside cottages, rural retreats, top-class hotels & villas. They provide a crèche, children's club, sporting facilities and 24 years of experience. Tel: 020 8541 2205; www.simplytravel.com

Corsican Places

This tour operator deals exclusively in Corsica, offering a range of accommodation from villas to coastal cottages to medieval village houses. They can arrange water sports and other activities on the island, and often have good late deals. Tel: 01903 748180; See www.corsica.co.uk

Voyages Ilena

Independent operator specialising in Corsican and Sardinian holidays, offering a variety of 'personally chosen' private villas, hotels and cottages in a range of locations throughout Corsica. Tel: 020 7924 4440; www.voyagesilena.co.uk

French Affair

An online provider of rental accommodation in various parts of France. In both Corsica and the Pays Basque they offer villas, cottages, mansions & village properties. Tel: 020 7381 8519; www.frenchaffair.com

Ascent Tours

U.S. based company offering eight day bicycle tours through the Pyrenees of the Pays Basque, staying in small family-run hotels, 'enjoying the countryside and local food'. www.ascenttours.com

Walkabout Gourmet

This enthusiastic Australian/European walking tour operator leads a 14-day Gastronomic Walk in the Pays Basque, from Biarritz into the Pyrenees sampling the best of the unique regional cuisine and a 9-day walk through the beautiful scenery of Corsica.
Web: www.walkaboutgourmet.com

Local Resources

There are an extraordinary number of websites on Corsica and the Basque Country to be found on the web, many of which are only available in French. The following is a small selection:

corsica-isula.com
A great directory-structure website - comprehensive, well-organised and in English, designed to provide all the possible information on Corsica that one could ever want. Listings for getting to Corsica, climate, geography, literature, festivals, music, the language, and numerous links to Corsican websites or foreign sites about Corsica.

allerencorse.com
Good French site, partly in English, with photos; maps; useful addresses (e.g. tourist offices, airports); ferry information; extensive direct links to hotel, campsite and property rental websites; links to boat hire companies and diving centres; exhaustive further links page.

corsica-net.com / corsica-online.com
Two multi-lingual sites sites with information to help potential tourists plan every aspect of their holiday.

corsica-guide.com
Good French only guide to hotels, campsites, restaurants, events,

sports, transports, practical info. Very extensive & well organised links page (mostly to French-only sites).

hotelscorse.com
Directory of 180 hotels and campsites in Corsica.

musee-fesch.com
Site of the Museum in Ajaccio with Napoleonic, early Italian and Baroque art collections.

home.nordnet.fr/~lbeaumadier
Personal site of Luc Beaumadier who has collated extensive resources on the Corsican railways, including history, photos, practical information and suggestions for tourists.

infobasque.com
Official website of the Pays Basque, listing information on the key regional towns and villages, hotels, campsites, festivals, language, sports, news, nature, history and more.

guide-basque.com
Unattractive, but well organised and useful French-only site with information and photos of Basque towns and villages, regional culture and traditions, local tourist sites, sporting possibilities, local webcams & good practical info on accommodation, transport, services.

touradour.com
Local Basque town information, history, hotels, transport, activities, maps, weather & links.

lebab.com
Practical Basque country information - cinema, restaurants, shopping, skiing, webcams, hotels.

bascoweb.com
Addresses and contact details for all local tourist offices in the Pays Basque.

euskadi.net
Official page of the Basque Government in Spain, which gives the background to the whole Basque nation, culture, history, language and current issues.

ville-biarritz.fr
Tourist board of Biarritz, with good general information on Basque country as well as more specific information on the town itself.

biarritzsurffestival.com
Everything you might need to know about surfing in Biarritz.

Hotel Choko Ona
Where Fraser Harrison stayed, overlooking the Landabat valley.
Avenue Harispe, 65210 Guethary; Tel: +33 05 59 26 51 01

Recommended Reading

Cadogan Guide to Corsica
Cadogan Guides. ISBN: 1-86011-962-X
Practical travel advice, photographs, maps, accommodation, eating & drinking, activities.

Landscapes Series : Corsica
by Noel Rochford. Sunflower Books. 2001 Edition (reprinted every 2 years)

The Basque History of the World
by Mark Kurlansky. Vintage. ISBN: 0099284138

Vacances: Basque Country
by Yasna Maznik. Cassell Guides. ISBN: 1842021591

The Dream-hunters of Corsica
by Dorothy Carrington ; Orion Paperbacks; ISBN: 1857994248

The Basque Kitchen: Tempting Food from the Pyrennees
by Gerald & Cameron Hirigoyen. HarperCollins Publishers. ISBN: 0067574610

Napoleon and His Parents : On the Threshold of History
by Dorothy Carrington ; E P Dutton; ISBN: 0525248331

Things to do 'Before You Die' No. 1001

Les Cents Cols
"Take your first steps towards joining the prestigious *Club des Cent Cols* (Club of the Hundred Peaks), hiking or biking amongst spectacular scenary. The best of these viewpoints are located on the watershed between the Mediterannean and the Atlantic." *Jamie Dunford Wood*

Cross-Channel France

Cross-Channel France

To the English, the lands across their channel means so much more than merely - or largely - being French. They represent Europe. However much you may try to persuade an Englishman that in this respect they are no different from ours, he will rarely accept the logic - at least not deep down. As a first glimpse of 'Europe' for us islanders, the coastal provinces of Brittany, Normandy and the Pas de Calais have a special place in our hearts.

For one thing, they are soaked in our blood. Most obviously, and visibly, in the cemeteries of the Somme and on the beaches of Gold and Sword, but also for centuries before that. Despite the Foreign Office's policy of avoiding continental military entanglements at all costs, at least prior to WWI, our armies were frequently landed in Calais, and all too frequently pulled out of there too. More than one invasion, and more than one threat of invasion, came from directly across these straits.

For many years large areas here were English, too, a legacy of the Norman conquest, Calais being the last part of continental Europe to be surrended apart from Gibraltar. We have strong genetic ties to the Normans, our continental cousins.

Moreover, when tourism was less highly developed than it is today, the extent of an average English person's experience of 'abroad' would have been a quick trip across the channel - where we found strange habits, insalubrious toilets, funny food and dangerous women - plenty to write home about, in fact.

Today, we continue to flock to these shores, now made so easy by the high speed ferries, the tempting supermarket shopping, and the Eurostar to Lille. The food and the habits have become familiar - revered in fact - and the sanitation has improved. Whether staying or simply passing through, as so many of us do, en route for the south, the coastal provinces seem as familiar as many parts of our own country. The landscape, too, of wet, green rolling hills, reminds us of home, which is why so many of us have chosen to settle or retire here. Familiar and close to home, yet foreign enough to be different, the lands across the Channel promise a standard of living and healthcare and schooling - a *quality* of life, for the moment at least - way superior to our own.

Christopher Somerville

THE SOMME

Shots were ringing out from the Bois D'Engremont, echoing across a shallow valley of cornfields now cut to stubble. "Local gun club," murmured Colonel David Church as he led us up the track towards the wood. Wry smiles flickered here and there among the party of walkers. The sound of gunfire here in the rolling landscape of northeast France, with the River Some flowing its sluggish course five miles to the south, held an irony we could well appreciate.

The Bois D'Engremont did not appear by name on the military map in my hand; it was labelled instead as "Bois Francais", the nickname by which the soldiers of Kitchener's army came to know and fear it. The gunfire that rattled among those trees at 7.30am on July 1, 1916 brought no smiles from the men of the 7th Green Howards and the 7th East Yorks, advancing towards a violent and horrible death as they attacked the village of Fricourt just over the ridge.

The Holt's Tours coach had dropped us off below the wood - 39 visitors from all areas of Britain, on the first evening of a four-day walking tour around the first world war battlefields of the Somme. Some were seasoned veterans of Holts' tours; two of our party had done more than 50 expeditions with the company, visiting battlefields all over the world from Waterloo to Gettysburg by way of Marathon. Others, like me, were rookies on our first tour, glad to absorb details of the Somme battles from professional experts such as Church and his co-guide, Isobel Swan, as well as drawing on the seemingly bottomless wells of information among our fellow travellers.

Standing under the trees by the grave of Corporal O'Brien, one among dozens of plain white headstones in the military cemetery of Citadel Camp, I learned from Tom Irving, a 50-tour veteran, the story of Siegfried Sassoon's heroic rescue of the corporal. "Sassoon went out to look for O'Brien, who'd been reported missing," Irving said. "He found him in a 25ft-deep crater, shot through both arms and legs. Sassoon sent for two strong men and a rope, and they got him out and back here to the camp. Sassoon got the Military Medal for that; but O'Brien died anyway." Later, back in England the disillusioned poet-soldier threw his medal into the River Mersey; he, like so many others who had been through the desperate experience of the Somme at the behest of generals and politicians far removed from the slaughter, could temporarily take no more. Yet Sassoon and most of those others returned to France to face the hellish scenes once again. What drove men such as these to such heights of endurance, and such depths of despair, was something I had come to France to get clearer in my own mind, here on the ground where they suffered.

On the edge of Bois Francais two big, rusting artillery shells stood on end under the trees, placed there by the farmer who had dug them up during the ploughing. Nearly eight decades after the battle, tons of unexploded ordnance are still unearthed each year from the chalk and clay of the Somme farmlands. "Shall I sit on one?" someone offered skittishly, posing for a photograph, "God, no," said her companion, sharply, "they're still live!" She gave a little scream and moved hastily away. Almost eighty years had passed since the shells thumped into the churned mud of the wood, but they still held a potent threat.

Fricourt lay clustered round its church spire beyond the ridge, a charming huddle of dark brick houses under red roofs. The village had been fortified German strongholds, spaced out along the 18-mile front where 100,000 men of the first attack wave climbed out of the British trenches and set off at a disciplined pace across no man's land into storms of machine-gun, sniper and shell fire.

At first, looking from the ridge across the sunlit sweep of peaceful woods and fields, it was hard to picture the setting at 7.30am on the July morning in 1916. But soon the battle scene, ingrained on my inner eye through reading and by images from flickering black and white cine films, sharpened into focus; Fricourt a mass of rubble, its countryside a wasteland of mud and splintered trees, shell holes and tangles of barbed wire into which the waves of attacking soldiers fell like scythed corn.

Now I could appreciate the lie of the land: how the German defenders commanded all the high ground, how the surrounding woods gave such excellent cover to their machine gunners; how this Somme country holds hidden dips and valleys that slowed the heavily laden British troops as they struggled uphill towards Fricourt. I knew from my reading that the Green Howards had lost 108 of the 140 men of A Company, that C and D Companies of the 7th East Yorks had lost 23 men in three minutes of the afternoon attack. Now, by seeing where, I could understand how.

Holts' Tours are congenial affairs. In the Novotel at Amiens that evening, the talk flowed over dinner and the wine flowed with it. There's nothing like walking in company for making friends of strangers, and there was plenty of leg-pulling about oversleeping and its relationship to good red wine when we boarded the coach next morning. As we drove south towards Maricourt, the starting point for our morning's walk, Church talked about the Pals battalions who had gone over the top side by side on this extreme right wing of the British attack: volunteers from towns around Liverpool and Manchester, friends and neighbours who would die or survive together.

Half a mile out of Maricourt, we crossed the line of the British trenches. "The sheer scale of the slaughter was what brought it home to people back in England," Church said as we walked between the quiet stubble and beet fields of no man's land, past German's Wood and Machine Gun Wood. "Hundreds were killed from the same few streets in the northern towns. After the Somme, the Pals battalions were discontinued."

Yet the Liverpool and Manchester pals of the 30th Division, volunteers to a man, achieved their objectives more successfully than any other unit along the entire battle front on that first day. They captured the ruins of Montauban and halted with a clear view over empty country beyond. There were no further orders to advance, however. They had suffered 3,011 casualties for the sake of a mile or so of devastated ground.

What made these drapers, clerks, railway porters and factory hands keep going as the machine-guns and artillery shells cut down their chums all around them? "It was the only thing they could do," said Church, "The safest place was in the German trench ahead of you. Get there, kick them out and take shelter - that was the incentive."

Among the fields of the Somme countryside are clusters of small woods, peaceful places today where finches and warblers sing. From mid-July 1916 onwards they became the splintered, leafless killing grounds for tens of thousands of British and German soldiers - Mametz Wood and Caterpillar Wood, Trones Wood, High Wood and Delville Wood, names the fighting men came to know all too well during that summer and autumn as the second Allied advance got under way.

Our afternoon walk took us to three of the woods, dark stands of oak, chestnut and ash that rustled in a gentle wind. This quiet whisper of thousands of leaves became the defining image of the Somme for me, an almost unbearably poignant sound.

Each wood had its own tranquil cemetery, crammed with headstones. There were more than 5,000 at Delville Wood; over 1,500 - including three pairs of brothers - at Flatiron Copse cemetery in Death Valley under Mametz Wood; nearly 4,000 at High Wood, where German machine-guns sliced down the Glasgow Highlanders as they tried day after day to penetrate the deadly shadows under the trees. High Wood temporarily scabious, I walked across a 300-yard strip of no man's land, still pockmarked with hundreds of shallow shell craters, towards the great brown caribou that lifts its bronze muzzle in a silent bellow above the trenches of the Ist Newfoundland Battalion. The Newfoundlanders were farmers, foresters and fishermen, men who had scarcely heard of France before they volunteered for service overseas. 752 went over the top together on July 1, 1916; 684 were killed or wounded.

I had learned a lot during these few days; but imagination had yet to cope with the still-unanswered question. What was it that kept the men of the Somme going forward, in a situation in which I could only imagine myself running abjectly away?

"They didn't whinge or mutiny," said Isobel Swan. "They went forward exhausted, soaked through, louse-ridden, in boots that didn't fit, to kill men they had no personal grudge against. Comradeship is an outmoded word, but that was the ideal they held - to look after the man next to you, share what you had with him, die for him if you had to."

She paused, then added simply: "They were better men than us."

Sadie Jones

THREE DAYS IN ARRAS

The journey from London to Normandy starts badly. The all too familiar M20, M23, M25 - how many motorways can one small island pack in? By the time you get to the European péage-style booths that are the approach to the Eurotunnel things appear to be looking up... until you hit the queues, the delays and ultimately the diversion to the ferries. Ferries which chug fatly over the heaving water like a kind of last oily breath of the seventies with their swirly carpets and nailed down tables. But then, just when you're beginning to think an economy seat to Australia next to a gastro-enteritic newborn would be preferable - France.

It was the damp tail-end of the year, that vacuum between Christmas and New Year and France was big and flat and pale grey-green. We (husband plus two small children) were dodging the whole London New Year thing and felt like naughty escapees. The drive from Calais to Arras is short and easy, just over an hour. Arras is a market town, a Cathedral city distinguished mainly by its Flemish architecture and its history. Surrounded by fairly featureless countryside, the city is built on a surprisingly big scale, the legacy of its once hugely important position as one of the great trading centres of Europe.

At first we fumbled for references. It's like Amsterdam; no, it's like Germany; no, England; a somewhat stolid place, friendly, welcoming but with what seemed to me a very Northern introversion. Businesslike, not frivolous.

Having read about the vast grey squares around which the city is built we left our luggage in our decidedly eccentric hotel room and dragged our resigned offspring towards the Grand Place. We had read of gabled buildings, cobbles, quietness and big sky - what we found was the entire square packed with cars, and crowds thronged behind the ropes strung along the pavements. There was an air of anticipation. German, Italian and Japanese crews and executives milled around laughing. It was the start of the Arras Dakar rally. Apparently the Paris Dakar rally has recently become the Arras Paris Dakar Rally - try saying that in a hurry. But by three in the morning they had all gone, roaring out of town past the chequered flag and through the cheering, roof slapping, singing crowd. And, like Portobello after Carnival, the next day it was as if none of it had ever been. One lonely puffy-jacketed bloke ate a late breakfast in the hotel dining room. Where's your motor? we wanted to shout across the white linen table cloths.

The style in these squares - the Grand Place, Place des Heros and behind the Gothic Hotel de Ville, the Place de la Vacquerie - is almost uniformly Flemish, while surrounding streets have a more classically French look. There are collonades, cheese shops, lingerie shops, crowded brasseries full of coffee, choucroute and red wine, cheese and fish shops and the amazing market that still fills nearly all of the three squares twice a week as it has done since the Middle Ages. The Saturday we were there it was packed with rows of stalls selling farm produce, clothing, live rabbits and chickens. Arras is all of that but also two things more; unique and fascinating things that lift it from a convenient second string short break destination to a 'must see' and what to me felt like an essential part of the European experience - not as in Millenium Dome Experience - as in the experience of being European...

During the 1914-1918 war the front line was just a few kilometres north-east of Arras. The city itself was occupied by German forces for three days in 1915 and endured devasting shelling for two and a half years after that. It was almost totally destroyed. So in 1918, when the war ended, the people undertook the most extensive restoration process ever attempted. They rebuilt the city from the rubble, pain-stakingly putting it back, brick by brick even, where possible, returning actual stones to their original buildings. A labour of love, successful, that has left the city almost as if the war had never been; instead of being a patchwork reminder of destruction it stands as a beautifully intact testimony to resilience.

Arras is built on limestone and since there was first a settlement here, in Roman times, the limestone has been used for something; it was quarried first of all and then, when the city grew, the tunnels of the quarries were used for storage. Now there are many kilometres of caves, or Boves, and still many more being discovered, they go down three levels, to a depth of 15 metres and run in a labyrinth of tunnels beneath all of the three squares. The cool, dry caves became wine cellars and dumps for the blue and white pottery and china that the area was once famous for; they were even used by Catholics as a place of worship during the Revolutionary Terror. It is hard to forget about the First War in Normandy and even the caves underneath Arras had their chilling part in it.

In 1916, when the city of Arras was on its knees and the front line had been pushed back and forth over the same few kilometres of mud for two years, 35,000 British troops arrived. According to a bilingual paper of the time, displayed in the boves, the local people gave the arriving soldiers a heros welcome. It was decided that the troops would be put into the caves and that parties of them would extend them, digging tunnels out beyond the town, beneath No-man's Land in order to literally come out of the ground and gain the advantage. So they lived underground, they slept, cooked, ate undergound with no ventilation for the oil lamps and stoves. They built huge caves with codenames like 'Devon' and 'Cornwall'. One of these, larger than the Grand Place itself, is now being turned into a museum forecast to open in 2004. The caves were used to put the wounded in too. We went on the short and informative guided tour of the caves; I expected ghosts, a lingering atmosphere of horror, but actually they felt safe, cosy, cool. Maybe they were a respite rather than a horror.

All around Arras there are signs for war cemeteries; English, French, German and Canadian, and it is the countryside that does seem haunted; if you've read any history of the first world war, or any poetry of the time, it's impossible not to picture it in this landscape. We went to the British cemetery on the edge of town, the largest British first world war cemetery in the area but surprisingly compact. It's amazing how many bodies you can pack in to a small space. Designed by Lutyens it resembles a large walled garden, the fourth wall being both the entrance and a tall neo-classical open courtyard and fountain. Only on closer examination do you see that this fourth wall, perhaps 18 feet high and 250 feet long, is entirely filled with the names of the dead whose bodies were never recovered; name, age and regiment. There are two thousand six hundred men in the ground and a further forty thousand names on the wall.

There is a terrible sadness and a stillness here, even with all the years that have passed. We walked up and down reading the names on the wall and the names on the immaculate gravestones while the children threw real snowballs at each other in the bright sunshine.

For a small place there's a lot to say about Arras. We were there for four nights and, not being too driven about filling our every moment with activity, we didn't have a chance to get to the Musee des Beaux-Arts which reportedly has amongst other things a rare collection of 18th century wall tapestries - those to which Arras gave its name (hence Polonious being slain whilst hiding behind one). Nor did we visit Robespierre's house; he was born in Arras and lived there for many years. Fantastically, the Maison Robespierre has recently been bought by a group of cycling enthusiasts who have apparently dedicated half of it to some sort of bicycle exhibition and the other half to Maximilien Robespierre, inventor of modern totalitarianism. All this and of course the thrilling Arras Paris Dakar Rally. Hey, I'd go back just for that.

Anthony Sattin

BRITTANY

There's no escaping seafood in Brittany, which isn't surprising since one half of France's entire seafood beds are found there, with oysters considered the prize. The raising of seafood is serious business, the eating of it a local obsession, so much so that even the amiable director of the tourist office in Morlaix admitted to eating at least a couple of dozen oysters each week.

"For my health, you understand," he said, the twinkle in his eye suggesting that it was also a pleasure.

In his office, I picked up a brochure which likened oysters to wine and divided Brittany's twelve centres of ostréiculture (oyster farming) into 'Grands Crus'. Morlaix was one of them, and Paimpol and Cancale, where we were headed, were among the most famous. The road we were taking could be called Brittany's oyster trail, its "route des huitres".

We arrived in Perros-Guirec, along the coast from Morlaix, in the evening and experienced the usual chaos of late arrival, the hurry to get bags out of the car, to wash and change and get the kids to a restaurant while there was still a vague chance they might eat. Along the waterfront, one of those typical northern Brittany inlets where a forest of yacht masts is surrounded by spreading development and sharp, tree-covered banks, we settled on a restaurant where huge platters of seafood were being carried in triumph out of the kitchen. For the next hour and more we became intimate with the fruits of what the French call *conchyliculture* (it gets easier after the first few attempts), with cockles and mussels, crabs, langoustines, whelks and prawns.

Our sons' fascination with the riches of the sea soon turned to disgust. But there was one thing missing: the oysters. It was 30 August and there is a rule that one shouldn't eat them during a month without an 'r' in it.

"But what difference can three days make?" I asked the waiter.

"You can have them if you want," he said with perfect French reserve. "But you will see that now they are still 'laiteuse', milky. Later they will be perfect."

The following morning we drove to Morlaix, ready to delight the kids with tales of pirates, princesses and great mariners, only to find the road blocked by modern-day pirates in the form of farmers and fishermen, protesting at fuel prices. "Come back after lunch," one of the tractor drivers suggested, so we followed the winding road along the Morlaix river to the sea. Carantec is the village there, a low-key resort backed up over rocks, its claim to fame being a quiet beach, a great view over the massive bay of Morlaix and a sailing tradition that led to the creation of the Optimist, now the world-standard boat for teaching beginners to sail.

Where parts of France's west coast have deep offshore canyons which throw huge waves onto the beach, much of Brittany's north coast is shallow. Just how shallow we were soon able to see, for by the time we were settled in the sand of Carantec beach, the water had receded far into the distance, boats were left high and dry and the seabed was revealed. And then another spectacle unfolded in front of us as an unlikely group followed the water out, some heavy men in wetsuits, retired couples with rakes, hoes and wicker

baskets and plenty of kids with nets and buckets. There was something ridiculous about the sight of all this gear - the picks, the waders, the floating baskets - and about the way they looked as though they were being drawn by a force greater than themselves. Later, curious as to what they had found, we went to inspect their baskets and found crabs and shrimps, winkles, snails, clams and what they call 'sea knives'. Then came a man with a bucket of oysters. "The other shells are good, but this," and he waved an oyster at me as though it was a wad of notes, "is the real treasure here."

It rained in the night, a sudden wind blowing a violent storm off the Atlantic, but the morning was all blue sky and sunshine. We hunted down a picnic lunch at Perros-Guirec market, then drove to Paimpol across a rugged peninsular of apple orchards, artichoke fields and tight villages of stone and slate. One hundred and fifty years ago, Paimpol was a major fishing port with a fleet that sailed to Iceland for cod and whales. Many of the old warehouses are now furniture stores and supermarkets, while a more genteel breed of sailor frequents the town, admiring the cut of his jib and telling tales not of Moby Dick but of cute inlets he spotted along the coast. The only sign of industry among all this leisure was some fishing boats and an old oyster dredger, squat and heavy among the streamlined yachts.

Looking for a place to picnic, we drove out of town and around the broad bay of Paimpol to Port Lazo, a small village huddled by a landing. From a granite perch along the shore, we spread out our meal in front of a clear view of the wide bay and retreating tide. Bunches of thick white cloud scudded overhead, gulls scavenged along the receding shore while the sun turned the sea blue, aquamarine, green, grey and many shades in between. Soon after we had finished eating, with the boys off hunting life in the rock pools and poles beginning to emerge from the water, a tractor came down the slip onto the beach.

Half an hour later there were five tractors, a large truck and a score of men on the beach, and the first of the oyster parks was beginning to emerge from the sea. Traditional oyster fishing involved dredging the seabed with rakes suspended off the sort of boat we had seen in Paimpol. Modern ostréiculture is a more certain enterprise, where sacks of baby oysters are strapped to tables, fixed onto the seabed and left to grow in the storming tides. What the farm workers have to do is ensure they have enough space to grow during the three to four years they take to reach maturity.

By the time I was on my feet, on the beach, the tide was so low that almost the entire bay had been drained, several acres of oyster parcs were exposed and Philippe, a local pensioner in boots and shorts, was out for his daily constitutional among the beds. With him were a Parisian friend, whom he mocked as a pampered townie, and his little lap dog, which he had to carry over the puddles. They were armed with sticks and buckets.

"We are not really supposed to come so close to the parcs, but I know one of the farmers here," Philippe explained, "and he lets me collect the oysters that fall."

From time to time he stopped to dig among the algae and plants and slimy sea floor and then dropped a creuse - curved, irregular - or, more rarely, a flat oyster into his bucket.

"It's a way of getting exercise and of eating well," and he patted his generous belly, though whether to show how fit he was or how well he ate I couldn't tell. Tossing another oyster into his bucket he laughed at his friend,

"How much do you pay for these in your Parisian restaurants, eh?" When I explained that some British restaurants charge up to a couple of pounds a piece, they both laughed.

"Here they are cheap, as they should be, because they are part of our heritage, our identity." And why? "This is the true taste of my country. More than the cider, the crepes and all that, it is the oysters of Paimpol. They have been eaten for as long as people have been living here."

I mentioned the brochure I had read about the different 'grands crus' along the coast.

"Exactly. And I can tell whether an oyster has come from Paimpol or Morlaix, even whether it has come from here or across the bay near Arcouest."

At this his Parisian friend scoffed and lit a Gauloise.

"The day I can't eat oysters," Philippe went on, swinging into improbable hyperbole, "is the day I shoot myself."

No wonder, I thought as I walked out of the sea, we go on about Gallic passion.

All afternoon we drove west along the wild, pirate coast, beneath alternate sun and cloud. By late afternoon we were in St. Malo, one of the greatest of corsair strongholds and Brittany's most visited attraction, its solid walls, arrow-slit towers and massive gates now hiding nothing more dangerous than a maze of shops and restaurants. It is also a place of natural spectacle and at the end of the day we ate crepes and drank cider watching the sun sink beneath the risen sea.

Cancale, just around the headland from St. Malo, has no pirate connections, but it has other reasons to blow its horn. Cancale is the mecca of ostréiculture - it is to oysters what Wall Street is to money and Milan to fashion. Oysters from Cancale were eaten by Julius Caesar, served daily at the table of Louis XIV and although he left his women behind, Napoleon made sure he took Cancale oysters with him on the road to Moscow. The town sits on the bay of Mont-Saint-Michael, the outline of the holy island visible some fifteen miles across the water. Between the two, the tide races in and out at many miles an hour each day. It is the strength of the tide and the richness of the water that makes Cancale the perfect oyster breeding ground.

But it's not all business. This is a pretty place, too, with a long waterfront and narrow harbour. And because of the success of its oysters, the town has become something of a gastronomic centre where Parisians will pop in for a weekend. And as a result, the seafront now has more eating options than you would expect in a town of some five thousand people, from small bars where you can scoff a dozen creuses with a glass of wine for a few pounds to the formal restaurant at Château Richeux, home to some of Brittany's fanciest cooking. We stayed; we ate.

I don't know if it was the cumulative effect of the few days we had spent along the coast, or the inspiration gleaned from our last lunch - a couple of dozen succulent, nutty, salty oysters bought from a stall at the little port, opened before our eyes and accompanied by a wedge of lemon. But when the tide was fully out, we too felt the force, the call of the sea and having pulled on boots, armed the kids with nets, taken a stick, a knife and some bags, we went to join the growing crowd of people scavenging along the shore.

Travel Specialists

Inntravel
Runs lots of short breaks to Flanders, Picardy and Normandy, suggesting interesting hotels and restaurants, cultural places to visit and a wide range of places to stay. Tel: 01653 629000; See www.inntravel.co.uk

Easy Breaks Brittany
For a selection of cycling, golfing and walking holidays of variable length. This French-based British couple offer both all-inclusive breaks such as the 'Ride & Ramble package' and self-drive options. Also has a number of gites available for hire. Tel: +33 297 39 34 83; See www.easy-breaksbrittany.com

Breton Bikes
Another ex-pat run local outfit, full of enthusiasm, testimonials and cycling tips. They offer cycling holidays for all age-ranges and abilities, staying in hotels or campsites. See www.bretonbikes.com

Normandie Vacances
List 120 self-catering gítes in Normandy. Tel: 01922 620278

Holts Tours - Battlefields and History
Specialists with over 20 years of experience in battlefield tours, generally on a half-board basis with travel between sites in coaches with experienced guides and guest speakers. Tel: 01304 612 248. See www.holts.co.uk

Local Resources

normandy-tourism.org
A well organised and comprehensive local tourism site covering all

aspects of visiting Normandy (such as accommodation, suggested places to visit etc.) with a good calendar of local events. Available in several languages.

bretagne.com
Brittany site, only available in French, but with great aerial views of local towns and villages & practical information on accommodation, trips, culture and services.

hotels-de-bretagne.com
Hotel guide to Brittany with additional information on local tourist offices, airports, events, and even casinos.

manchetourisme.com
Official site of the Manche Tourist Board (The most westerly department of Normandy) listing accommodation, what to see & visit, events, news, photos, restaurants, activities and contact details for all local tourist offices.

lilletourism.com
Official website of Lille's tourist board, for good general information on Lille and region.

ot-arras.fr
Local tourist board website for the town of Arras.

Recommended Reading

Cadogan Guide to Brittany by Phillipe Barbour. Cadogan Books. ISBN: 1-86011-044-4
For insight into Breton history, culture, accommodation, food, trips and islands.

Holiday Walks in Brittany / **Holiday Walks in Normandy** by Judy Smith. Sigma Leisure. ISBN: 1850587337 / 1850587361

On the Road Around Normandy, Brittany and the Loire Valley: Driving Holidays in Northern France
by Roger Thomas, Lucy Koserski. Passport Books.
ISBN: 0844290114

The Most Beautiful Villages of Brittany by James Bentley, Hugh Palmer. Thames and Hudson. ISBN: 0500019355

Normandy, Picardy & Pas de Calais by Barbara Eperon.
A & C Black Publishers.

Major and Mrs Holt's Battlefield Guide to Normandy by Tonie & Valmai Holt. Pen & Sword Books / Leo Cooper.
ISBN: 0850526620

A Traveller's Guide to D-Day and the Battle for Normandy by Carl Shilleto, Mike Tolhurst. Cassell Illustrated. ISBN: 1900624354

Last Word

It's Pavlovian. Pure and simple. Say Lyon and I see snug wooden booths, steamed-up windows and paper squares diamond-draped over red gingham tablecloths. The wine arrives in a pot - that heavy-bottomed glass carafe with a rubber band around its neck for every refill you order - and the food is served in workmanlike proportions, the kind of helpings you'd expect after digging up a road or ploughing a field. An immediate, irresistable response. Simply Pavlovian.

A perfect day in Lyon, for me, revolves around food - not inappropriate in the gastronomic heart of France - preferably sometime in late October when caramel-coloured leaves skitter along the sidewalks and river mists rise over tree-lined quais to shroud the city streets. It's a grand time to be there because the snap makes you walk fast and gets the blood pumping. Which is a good feeling. Nothing summery or slothful. It also helps work up an appetite.

MORNING

In any city it's good to start with a view, somewhere to get your bearings. There are those who'll recommend the belevedere at the Basilique Notre-Dame de Fourviere, the place Rouville or rue des Fantasques but for my money it has to be the terrace of the sumptuous Villa Florentine on Montée Saint-Barthélémy, taking my coffee, brioche pralinée and perhaps a guilty calva perched above the rosy, pantiled roofs of Vieux Lyon. These ochre-ish, umber-ish teetering, turretted buildings comprise one of the most remarkable renaissance districts anywhere in Europe, real history on the hoof, an extraordinary abundance of princely palaces and merchant mansions, tunnelled with an echoing warren of stone-vaulted medieval passageways called 'traboules' that link one street to another.

But on my perfect day there's another destination I have in mind, somewhere best approached in the early hours, across the Soane and the Rhone at whose confluence this city lies. I'm headed for Les Halles de la Part-Dieu on the corner of rue Garibaldi and cours Lafayette, a vast concrete cathedral devoted to all things edible and some, by the look of them, not so edible. Here, for me, are the real treasures of the city and its surroundings: fat-veined cuts of Charolais beef, puckered blankets of creamy tripe and tubs of jellied brawn, those celebrated poulets de Bresse with their heads tucked sleepily under their wings, marble slabs of gold-scaled carp and pike from the Dombes lakeland, feathery, furry pelmets of dead-eyed game, straw-plattered local cheeses and everywhere those grossly swollen, tightly corseted saucissons de Lyons. For me there's no better way to get the juices flowing than a stroll through Lyon's larder.

LUNCH

But where to go, which particular table to take in this city of tables? My advice, come lunchtime, is look for a wheatsheaf painted beside a door and find yourself a bouchon, the traditional Lyonnais bistro named after the straw plugs once used as bottle-stoppers. Here the food is prix fixe and plentiful - a bowl of pumpkin soup or plate of local charcuterie, a roti de porc or pavé de boeuf served with pommes Lyonnais the colour of old ivory, finished off with a round of St Marcellin affiné washed down with a rough little local rouge served in the obligatory pot. On my perfect day you'll find me at Chez Sylvain on rue Tapin, La Meuniere on rue Neuve or Raymond Fulchiron's venerable Café des Fédérations on rue du Major-Martin with its football team photos and club pennants, those steamed-up windows, red-chequered tablecloths and bustling, smokey hum.

Afternoon

With something to walk off, there's no shortage of suitable digestifs. I could climb the Croix-Rousse hill where Lyon's 30,000 silk weavers (or canuts) worked their nineteenth-century looms to a deafening 'bistanclac-bistanclac' sound-track, snacking on a bag of salty roast chestnuts or the roadside crepes called matefaim for which this district is also celebrated. Or I could head for the Musée des Beaux-Arts, accommodated in an old Benedictine convent on place des Terreaux, stepping cautiously past Daniel Buren's timed waterspouts to search out two thousand years of foodie still lifes.

More likely though I'll set off south, a self-indulgent stroll down the length of Presqu'ile, the aptly-name peninsula that separates the Soane and the Rhone, to rue de la Charité and the Musée Historiques des Tissus and the Musée des Arts Decoratifs. Unlike the Beaux-Arts they're conveniently compact and accessible - one ticket for both, a steal. From here it's an easy amble past the tantalising, dream-on antique shops of rue Auguste-Comte where any retail therapy is likely to entail a mortgage, over the grand expanse of place Bellecour where they play Albinoni adagios in the underground car park and back across the Soane to the cobbles and stone quais of Vieux Lyon.

Evening

With a night sky looming over the distant alps and sliding across the Dauphiné plain, it's that rock and a hard place again. What to choose? Where to go? A night at the opera back in Presqu'ile under the barrel-vaulted glass roof of Jean Nouvel's stunning new opera house? Or, since it's my perfect day, trust to the elements on a stone seat for an open-air concert in the smaller of Lyon's two Roman amphitheatres, the spot where this city started out more than two thousand years ago? A communard, a glass of the local beaujolais mixed with créme de cassis, aids the decision-making and I opt for those open spaces.

And then, you guessed it, dinner. A little more formal this time, a little more elevated to suit the evening's entertainment - La Mere Brazier on rue Royale perhaps, or Léon de Lyon on rue Pléney, or Pierre Orsi on place Kléber or, further afield, Alain Chapel at Mionnay, Paul Bocuse at Collonges-au-Mont d'Or or the spoiling tables of Chateau de Bagnols. In the end, though, it's a familiar, anticipatory wander along rue du Boeuf where Philippe Chavent's La Tour Rose is waiting to seduce and delight with an oyster soup sprinkled with caviar, quennelles soft as shaving foam, illicitly pink magrets and steaming beignets soufflées fourrés aux cerises. And I don't even have to wear a tie.

Call me a philistine, but I can't imagine a more perfect day.

ALF ALDERSON is a freelance journalist specialising in adventure travel, and his work has appeared in The Guardian, Daily Telegraph, Condé Nast Traveller, Mail on Sunday, The Independent, Times Educational Supplement, Time Out and Global Adventure. He has also appeared in adventure sports programmes for the BBC, Sky TV and American cable networks.

MAUREEN BARRY has contributed regular travel, food and wine features to British Airways Highlife magazine for twelve years, as well as contributing to other titles in the Premier group, national magazines and newspapers. She is a partner in an Internet Information company and writes regularly for the web. She holds a BA degree in Russian and French from London University and has one published novel, 'Brilliant'.

RICHARD BINNS is the pre-eminent writer of travel guides to France and Britain, including the renowned 'French Leave' series. Most of his 17 self-published guides have been bestsellers; one made the No. 1 spot in both The Sunday Times and The Times lists. For 20 years he has contributed regularly to national newspapers and magazines, including over 100 articles for The Sunday Times alone. He is the only travel writer to have won a France Travelaureat, an award nominated by the 60,000-plus subscribers to the highly acclaimed France magazine. He has also been awarded La Medaille d'Argent du Tourisme by the French Government.

ANDREW EAMES started in journalism in Southeast Asia as a contributor to the Straits Times. In the UK, he edited magazines Frontier and Business Traveller and was Executive Editor of guidebook publisher Insight Guides before going freelance. He writes regularly for the travel sections of the Times, Independent, Evening Standard, Daily Mail and Daily Express, and for magazines such as HighLife and Food & Travel. Besides a raft of guidebooks edited for Insight Guides, his own personal books include two travel autobiographies, 'Crossing the Shadow Line' and 'Four Scottish Journeys' (both published by Hodder & Stoughton); 'Four Scottish Journeys' was serialized by BBC Radio Four.

JUSTINE HARDY was born in England and trained as a journalist in Australia. She is also an author and documentary-maker; her titles include 'The Ochre Border: A Journey through the Tibetan Frontierlands' (1995); 'Scoop-Wallah: Life on a Delhi Daily' (1999) and 'Goat: A Story about Kashmir and Notting Hill' (2000).

FRASER HARRISON has written eight books, as well as reviews and articles for a wide variety of magazines and papers, including the travel section of The Sunday Times. He has recorded many essays and features for BBC Radio. In 2001 he completed an MA in human rights at Essex University and now works for the Refugee Legal Centre. He lives in Helions Bumpstead, Essex with his wife.

JAMES HENDERSON has contributed to the Travel Pages of the Financial Times and other broadsheets for the past ten years, and is author of The Cadogan Guide to the Caribbean and the Bahamas, now in its fifth edition.

SADIE JONES is a Jamaica-born London-based scriptwriter and inveterate traveller. She spent a year in Paris since when she has developed a deep love of the country, marrying in St. Paul de Vence. Her dream however remains - to ride an Arab pony over the Himalayas...

JIM KEEBLE writes regularly for the travel pages of the UK's Daily and Sunday Telegraph, the Times and Sunday Times and the London Evening Standard. His first book, 'Independence Day - travels around America with a broken heart' was published by Abacus. He writes about anywhere that offers strange stories and frothy cocktails, in particular the Mediterranean and the Americas.

MARTIN O'BRIEN is a British-based freelance journalist and photographer. Formerly travel editor at Vogue (UK) and Editorial Director for UPL Films in London and Los Angeles, he has contributed travel features to a variety of newspapers and magazines worldwide. In the UK Martin has written for Condé Nast Traveller, The Daily Mail, Mail on Sunday, Elle and Time; in Australia for Vogue, Playboy and

Mode and in the US Four Seasons Magazine, European Travel & Life and British Living & Style. His photo-stories have also appeared in Conde Nast Traveller and Vogue. He has published two books; '60 Years of Travel in Vogue' (1980) and 'All The Girls' (1982), described by Auberon Waugh as "A classic among travel books."

ANTHONY SATTIN is a writer, critic and broadcaster. He is the author of several books including a novel 'Shooting the Breeze', and the highly acclaimed 'The Pharaoh's Shadow', the subject of a Radio 4 documentary. He has written for television, radio and for numerous publications in the UK and abroad and is a regular contributor to the Sunday Times books and travel pages.

DAN SCOTT is an award-winning freelance travel writer now based in Europe after seven years working in Australia. He specialises in adventure travel stories and has spent a lot of time in the Outback of Australia, and recently researched and wrote a guide book to the Kimberley region for Australian Geographic. He also writes frequently on diving in such locations as Tahiti, Milford Sound in New Zealand and off the coasts of Australia.

CHRISTOPHER SOMERVILLE is one of the UK's most respected freelance travel writers. His 'Walk of the Month' feature has been running in the Daily Telegraph for ten years, and his travel pieces appear regularly in Britain's top-quality newspapers - the Daily and Sunday Telegraph, the Times and the Sunday Times. Christopher has written around 20 books - some accounts of his travels, several walking guides, and guidebooks to the UK, Ireland and Crete. Broadcasting activity includes researching, writing and presenting his own long-running 'Somerville's Walks' series on TV, and a varied experience of radio which now includes presenting a monthly walk on BBC Radio 4's travel programme 'Excess Baggage'.

LUCRETIA STEWART was born in Singapore and educated in Ankara, Peking, Washington D.C. and England. She has worked extensively as a journalist, and is the author of 'Tiger Balm: Travels in Laos, Vietnam & Cambodia' (1992); 'The Weather Prophet: A Caribbean Journey'

(1995), which was short-listed for the 1996 Thomas Cook Travel Book Award, and 'Making Love: A Romance' (1999), and the editor of 'Erogenous Zones: An Anthology of Sex Abroad' (2000). Lucretia was commissioning editor at Granta from 1998-1990 and she remains a contributing editor to the magazine.

STANLEY STEWART's books include 'Old Serpent Nile', an account of his journey from the mouth to the source of the White Nile, and 'Frontiers Of Heaven', about his journey across China from Shanghai to the Karakoram. The latter won the Thomas Cook/Daily Telegraph Travel Book Award. His most recent book is 'In The Empire Of Genghis Khan', the story of a thousand mile ride across Mongolia. He writes regularly for the Daily Telegraph and the Sunday Times where his work has won a clutch of awards.

NIGEL TISDALL: On a grey Monday morning in 1985 Nigel Tisdall went to London's Liverpool Street station and caught a train to China - you only have to change seven times and you're in Hong Kong. Afterwards he sold some stories about his trip to the Guardian and Sunday Times, and he has been a travel writer and photographer ever since. As well as contributing to numerous UK-based newspapers and magazines including the Times, Daily Telegraph and Elle, Tisdall has contributed to various travel guides published by Insight, AA and Dorling Kindersley featuring destinations such as Seville, Brittany, Madeira and California. He has also worked as the Travel Editor for Elle Decoration and Red magazines.

A recipient of many awards for travel writing, Tisdall currently writes regularly for the Daily Telegraph, Sunday Telegraph, London Evening Standard and Condé Nast Traveller.

ACKNOWLEDGEMENTS

The Luberon was first published in 'High Life Magazine'.
Is There Glamour Left For Tea? was first published in the Daily Telegraph.

Picture Credits